We have designed this guide with both Foundation and Higher level candidat~~~ ~~~~~~~~~ It includes:

- Foundation material in BLUE.

- Higher material in GREEN.

- Grammar sections in RED, integrated into the main section of the booklet so that you can see how the points we cover apply to a particular topic.

- A mini-test at regular intervals to enable you to assess how your revision is going.

- A section on exam technique.

- A grammar summary.

    The guide is intended for use with any GCSE specification.

CONSULTANT EDITOR ...

- **Debbie Hill** - Former Head of Modern Languages at Magdalen College School, Brackley.

CONTENTS

GRAMMAR CONTENTS

This guide is intended to consolidate what you have learnt throughout your course and to refresh your memory as you approach your exams.

- Use our mini-tests to constantly test yourself ... WITHOUT LOOKING AT THE BOOK!

- Don't just read, learn actively! Talk to yourself in German, record yourself, work with a friend, write things down.

- When you have revised a section, tick the boxes on the contents page, this will help you to see how your revision is progressing.

- Jot down anything which will help you to remember, no matter how trivial.

- Remember that our vocabulary lists don't include everything. Use your dictionary to add to them.

- Remember that if you are entered for different levels in the different skills you will need to use both Foundation and Higher level material.

Spelling Reforms

NEW GERMAN SPELLING REFORMS

This guide incorporates the new German spelling reforms now accepted by all the German Länder and all German-speaking countries.

Some of the main differences are:

- The use of ss instead of ß after a short vowel sound:
  - e.g. dass instead of daß
  - muss instead of muß

- Some verb combinations have changed:
  - e.g. spazierengehen now spazieren gehen
  - kennenlernen now kennen lernen

- And other word combinations:
  - e.g. wieviel now wie viel

- Some changes in the use of capital letters:
  - e.g. es tut mir leid now es tut mir Leid

Grammar

To get a good **GCSE** grade you must have a sound understanding of the rules of German grammar, and be able to apply these rules in your own spoken and written German. Throughout this guide we have tried to show you points of grammar in the context of a particular topic. Where this has not been possible, grammar points have been included in the Grammar Summary on pages 81 to 91.

You will need to know the following grammatical terms:

1. Noun - the name of an object or person or place.
   e.g. der Hund, die Schweiz, das Mädchen

2. Singular and Plural - a singular noun means there is only one thing or person, a plural noun means there is more than one.
   e.g. singular die Katze, das Haus
   plural die Katzen, die Häuser

3. Pronoun - used in place of a noun.
   e.g. Der Mann lacht. Er lacht (Er (he) is the pronoun replacing der Mann).

4. Adjective - a "describing" word, giving more information about a noun.
   e.g. eine schwarze Katze
   blonde Haare

5. Verb - a "doing" word, indicating the actions of people or things.
   e.g. Er spielt Tennis

6. Subject - of a verb is the person or thing "doing the verb."
   e.g. Ich esse einen Apfel (ich is the subject of the verb).

7. Direct Object - of a verb is the person or thing which is having something done to it.
   e.g. Ich esse einen Apfel (einen Apfel is the direct object of the verb).

8. Indirect Object - of a verb usually has "to" or "for" in front of it.
   e.g. Ich gebe meinem Bruder (indirect object) einen Apfel (direct object).

9. Infinitive - the form of the verb found in the dictionary meaning "to do something."
   e.g. spielen (to play); geben (to give).

10. Tense - of a verb tells you when the action takes place - in the past, present or future.

11. Adverb - describes a verb, often explains "how", "when" or "where."
    e.g. Sie spricht schnell

12. Preposition - describes the position of a person or thing.
    e.g. vor dem Kino

Foundation

0 - null	10 - zehn	20 - zwanzig	30 - dreißig
1 - eins	11 - elf	21 - einundzwanzig	31 - einunddreißig
2 - zwei	12 - zwölf	22 - zweiundzwanzig	40 - vierzig
3 - drei	13 - dreizehn	23 - dreiundzwanzig	50 - fünfzig
4 - vier	14 - vierzehn	24 - vierundzwanzig	60 - sechzig
5 - fünf	15 - fünfzehn	25 - fünfundzwanzig	70 - siebzig
6 - sechs	16 - sechzehn	26 - sechsundzwanzig	80 - achtzig
7 - sieben	17 - siebzehn	27 - siebenundzwanzig	90 - neunzig
8 - acht	18 - achtzehn	28 - achtundzwanzig	100 - (ein)hundert
9 - neun	19 - neunzehn	29 - neunundzwanzig	101 - hundert(und)eins

200 -	zweihundert
250 -	zweihundert(und)fünfzig
1,000 -	(ein)tausend
2,000 -	zweitausend
1,000,000 -	eine Million
2,000,000 -	zwei Millionen

To change 1 to 1st, 2 to 2nd etc add 'te' to numbers up to and including 19, and add 'ste' to numbers 20 and above:

2 to 2nd — zwei to zweite
4 to 4th — vier to vierte
20 to 20th — zwanzig to zwanzigste

NOTE the exceptions to this rule:
1 to 1st — eins to erste
3 to 3rd — drei to dritte
7 to 7th — sieben to siebte
8 to 8th — acht to achte

All ordinal numbers in German must agree with the noun:
der erste Mann - the first man
die dritte Straße - the third street
ein zweites Haus - a second home

See page 11 and page 84.

Vocabulary

Die Tage der Woche - Days of the week

Montag - Monday
Dienstag - Tuesday
Mittwoch - Wednesday
Donnerstag - Thursday
Freitag - Friday
Samstag - Saturday
Sonntag - Sunday
am Montag - on Monday(s)
montags - on Mondays

Die Monate - Months of the Year

Januar - January
Februar - February
März - March
April - April
Mai - May
Juni - June
Juli - July
August - August
September - September
Oktober - October
November - November
Dezember - December

Die Jahreszeiten - The Seasons

der Frühling - Spring
der Sommer - Summer
der Herbst - Autumn
der Winter - Winter
im Frühling - in Spring
im Sommer - in Summer
im Herbst - in Autumn
im Winter - in Winter

Das Datum - The Date

Welches Datum haben wir heute?
Den wievielten haben wir heute? } - What's the date today?

There are two possibilities when giving the date in German:
heute ist der neunte November (nominative case)
heute haben wir den neunten November (accusative)

Foundation

Make sure that you can spell out loud in German, particularly your name.

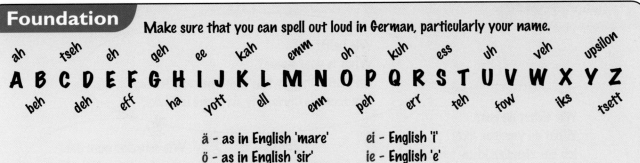

ah	tseh	eh	geh	ee	kah	emm	oh	kuh	ess	uh	veh	upsilon
A	**B C D**	**E F**	**G H**	**I J**	**K L**	**M N**	**O P**	**Q R**	**S**	**T U**	**V W**	**X Y Z**
beh	deh	eff	ha	yott	ell	enn	peh	err	teh	fow	iks	tsett

ä - as in English 'mare'   ei - English 'i'
ö - as in English 'sir'   ie - English 'e'
ü - as in English - 'queue'

Telling The Time

Uhr - (o'clock)
Mittag - (midday)
Mitternacht - (midnight)

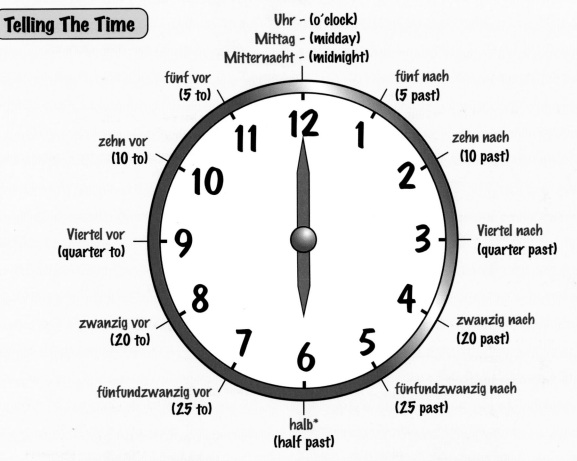

fünf vor (5 to)
fünf nach (5 past)
zehn vor (10 to)
zehn nach (10 past)
Viertel vor (quarter to)
Viertel nach (quarter past)
zwanzig vor (20 to)
zwanzig nach (20 past)
fünfundzwanzig vor (25 to)
fünfundzwanzig nach (25 past)
halb* (half past)

Wie spät ist es? - What time is it?
Um drei Uhr - at 3 o'clock
um halb sechs - at half past <u>five</u>

Wann?/Um wie viel Uhr? - When?/at what time?
um Viertel nach vier - at a quarter past 4
um Mitternacht - at Midnight

* halb vier - half past three
In German you refer to the coming hour i.e. half an hour to four

You need to be familiar with both the 12 and the 24 hour clock in German.

a.m.

1.00 es ist ein Uhr

2.00 es ist zwei Uhr

7.00 es ist sieben Uhr

10.00 es ist zehn Uhr

p.m.

13.00 es ist dreizehn Uhr

14.00 es ist vierzehn Uhr

19.00 es ist neunzehn Uhr

22.00 es ist zweiundzwanzig Uhr

Foundation

Wie heißt du?
What is your name?
Ich heiße Chris. Mein Familienname ist Taylor.
My name is Chris. My surname is Taylor.

Wie siehst du aus?
What do you look like?
Ich bin ziemlich klein. Ich habe dunkle Haare und braune Augen.
I'm quite small. I have dark hair and brown eyes.

Wie schreibt man das?
How do you spell that?
T-A-Y-L-O-R.

Wie alt bist du? How old are you?
Ich bin sechzehn Jahre alt.
I'm 16 years old.

Wo bist du geboren?
Where were you born?
Ich bin in Northampton geboren.
I was born in Northampton.

Wann hast du Geburtstag?
When is your birthday?
Ich habe am vierzehnten Mai Geburtstag.
My birthday is on the 14th May.

Wie ist deine Telefonnummer?
What is your telephone number?
Meine Telefonnummer ist dreiundsechzig, einundsiebzig, null acht.
My telephone number is 637108

Wo wohnst du?
Where do you live?
Ich wohne in Leeds.
I live in Leeds.

Wie ist deine Adresse?
What is your address?
Meine Adresse ist Park Avenue vierundzwanzig.
My address is 24 Park Avenue.

Vocabulary

das Geburtsdatum	-	date of birth
der Geburtsort	-	place of birth
der Wohnort	-	place of residence
die Adresse ⎫ die Anschrift ⎭	-	address
das Alter	-	age
der Familienstand	-	marital status
ledig	-	single
verheiratet	-	married
getrennt	-	separated
geschieden	-	divorced
der Beruf	-	profession
der Student/die Studentin	-	student (m/f)
der Schüler/die Schülerin	-	pupil (m/f)
die Staatsangehörigkeit	-	nationality
die Postleitzahl	-	postcode
die Vorwahlnummer	-	area dialling code
der Vorname	-	first, Christian name
der Familienname ⎫ der Nachname ⎭	-	surname
aussehen	-	to look
wie sieht er aus?	-	what does he look like?
der Bart	-	beard
der Schnurrbart	-	moustache
eine Brille tragen	-	to wear glasses

er trägt eine Brille	-	he wears glasses
faul	-	lazy
fleißig	-	hard-working
freundlich	-	friendly
glücklich	-	happy
intelligent	-	intelligent
lustig	-	funny, amusing
(for more character descriptions see p.10)		
groß	-	tall
klein	-	small
mittelgroß	-	average height
lang	-	long
kurz	-	short
glatt	-	straight
lockig	-	curly
blond	-	blond
schlank	-	slim
dünn	-	thin
dick	-	fat
hübsch	-	pretty
gutaussehend	-	good-looking
schön	-	nice, pretty
hässlich	-	ugly

Higher

At Higher level you need to recognise, and also use, language that is more complex and aim for greater accuracy, fluency and variety of vocabulary.

Seit wann wohnst du in Leeds?
How long have you been living in Leeds?
Ich wohne seit elf Jahren hier.
I have lived here for 11 years.

Was für ein Mensch bist du?
What kind of person are you?
Ich bin ziemlich schüchtern, sympathisch und immer ehrlich, aber manchmal bin ich egoistisch.
I'm fairly shy, friendly and always honest, but sometimes I'm selfish.

Grammar

The Present Tense

Regular (weak) verbs in the present tense have the following endings:

ich wohne	-	I live, do live, am living
du wohnst	-	you live, do live, are living
er/sie/es wohnt	-	he/she/it lives, does live, is living
wir wohnen	-	we live, do live, are living
ihr wohnt	-	you live, do live, are living
Sie wohnen	-	you live, do live, are living
sie wohnen	-	they live, do live, are living

Note that the verb endings will change according to the subject pronouns:

Ich (I), du (you, singular and informal), er (he, it), sie (she, it), es (it), wir (we), ihr (you, plural of du), Sie (you, polite form, singular and plural), sie (they).

Two very common but IRREGULAR verbs in the present tense are HABEN - to have and SEIN - to be:

HABEN			SEIN		
Ich habe	-	I have	ich bin	-	I am
du hast	-	you have	du bist	-	you are
er/sie/es hat	-	he/she/it has	er/sie/es ist	-	he/she/it is
wir haben	-	we have	wir sind	-	we are
ihr habt	-	you have	ihr seid	-	you are
Sie/sie haben	-	you/they have	Sie/sie sind	-	you/they are

Mini Test

1. Say as much as you can about yourself in German, without looking at this guide. Record it onto cassette and time yourself.
2. Play back the tape, see if you can correct your own mistakes and add 5 more details.
3. Practise form-filling. Write out the various headings in German, and without reference to this guide, fill in the form.

Foundation

Was ist dein Vater/ deine Mutter von Beruf?
What does your father/ mother do?
Mein Vater ist Hotelmanager.
Meine Mutter ist Ärztin.
My father is a hotel manager. My mother is a doctor.

Wie viele Personen gibt es in deiner Familie?
How many people are there in your family?
Wir sind fünf - meine Mutter, mein Vater, mein Bruder, meine Schwester und ich.
There are 5 of us - my mother, my father, my brother, my sister and myself.

Hast du Geschwister?
Have you got any brothers or sisters?
Ja, ich habe einen Bruder und eine Schwester/ja, ich habe 2 Brüder und 2 Schwestern/nein, ich bin Einzelkind.
Yes, I've got one brother and one sister/ yes, I've got 2 brothers and 2 sisters/ no, I'm an only child.

Hast du Haustiere?
Have you any pets?
Ja, wir haben eine Katze. Sie heißt Tiddles, und ist sehr süß/Nein, wir haben keine Haustiere.
Yes, we've got a cat called Tiddles and she is really sweet/No, we haven't got any pets.

Kannst du deinen Bruder/deine Schwester beschreiben?
Can you describe your brother/sister?
Er/mein Bruder/sie/meine Schwester ist ziemlich klein und hat blaue Augen und kurze blonde Haare.
He/my brother/she /my sister is quite small, and has blue eyes and short blond hair.

(See p.26 for list of professions)

Vocabulary

DIE FAMILIE	-	THE FAMILY
der Vater	-	father
die Mutter	-	mother
der Bruder	-	brother
die Schwester	-	sister
der Sohn	-	son
die Tochter	-	daughter
Zwillinge	-	twins
die Eltern	-	parents
die Großeltern	-	grandparents
der Großvater/Opa	-	grandfather
die Großmutter/Oma	-	grandmother
der Enkel/die Enkelin	-	grandson/grandaughter
der Onkel	-	uncle
die Tante	-	aunt
der Cousin / der Vetter	-	male cousin
die Kusine	-	female cousin
der Mann	-	man, husband
die Frau	-	woman, wife
das Kind	-	child
das Baby	-	baby
der Junge	-	boy
das Mädchen	-	girl
der/die Verwandte	-	relation

HAUSTIERE	-	PETS
der Hund	-	dog
die Katze	-	cat
das Kaninchen	-	rabbit
das Meerschweinchen	-	guinea pig
das Pferd	-	horse
der Wellensittich	-	budgerigar
der Goldfisch	-	goldfish
der Hamster	-	hamster
die Schildkröte	-	tortoise
die Maus	-	mouse
frech	-	cheeky
neugierig	-	curious, nosy
lebhaft	-	lively
gut/schlecht gelaunt	-	good/bad tempered
schüchtern	-	shy
sympathisch	-	kind, nice
ehrlich	-	honest
egoistisch	-	selfish
ein bisschen	-	a little, a bit
ziemlich	-	quite
sehr	-	very
immer	-	always
sich gut verstehen mit / gut auskommen mit	-	to get on well with
sich streiten	-	to argue

Higher

Erzähle mir ein bisschen von deiner Familie.
Tell me a bit about your family.
(A request like this at Higher level would expect you to put together the information on the previous page with little or no prompting).

Sag mir etwas über den Charakter deiner Schwester.
Tell me about your sister's personality.
Meine Schwester ist unheimlich frech, sehr lebhaft und manchmal schlecht gelaunt.
My sister is incredibly cheeky, very lively and sometimes bad tempered.

Kommst du mit deiner Familie gut aus?
Do you get on well with your family?
Ich verstehe mich gut mit meinen Eltern, aber ich streite mich oft mit meinem Bruder - wir sind uns zu ähnlich.
I get on well with my parents, but I often argue with my brother - we're too alike.

Grammar

Adjectives

When an adjective stands alone, i.e. FOLLOWS the object it is describing, it does not require an ending:

e.g. meine Schwester ist frech - **my sister is cheeky**
dein Bruder ist groß und schlank - **your brother is tall and slim**

When the adjective stands in front of the object it is describing, an ending is required :

e.g. Sie hat lange blonde Haare und blaue Augen - **she has long, blond hair and blue eyes**
Wir haben einen großen schwarzen Hund zu Hause - **we've got a big, black dog at home.**
The endings will depend on the GENDER and the CASE of the object described.

(For more information on adjective endings see Grammar Summary page 84)

Possessive Adjectives

As the name suggests, these are adjectives which denote possession of something.

mein	-	my	Because these are ADJECTIVES, endings must be added
dein	-	your	according to the gender of the object possessed, and the case e.g.
sein	-	his, its	mein Bruder ist faul **my brother is lazy**
ihr	-	her, its	mein Bruder = **masculine nominative**
sein	-	its	hast du seinen Bruder gesehen? **Did you see his brother?**
unser	-	our	seinen Bruder = **masculine accusative**
euer	-	your	wir haben mit unserer Deutschlehrerin gesprochen
Ihr	-	your	**we spoke to our German teacher**
ihr	-	their	mit unserer Deutschlehrerin = **feminine dative dependant on 'mit'**

Mini Test

1. Talk for 2 minutes in German about your family and pets. Record yourself on tape.
2. Think of 5 questions you might ask someone in German about their family.

Foundation

Spielst du in einer Band
oder in einem Orchester?
Do you play in a band
or an orchestra?
Ich spiele Gitarre in
einer Schulband.
I play the guitar in
a school band.

Was für Hobbys hast du?
What hobbies do you have?
Meine Hobbys sind Sport und Radfahren.
My hobbies are sport and cycling.

Treibst du gern Sport?
Do you enjoy sport?
Ja, ich spiele gern Basketball und Fußball.
Yes, I enjoy playing basketball and football.

Spielst du ein Instrument?
Do you play a musical instrument?
Ja, ich spiele Gitarre und Keyboard.
Yes, I play the guitar and keyboard.

Spielst du in einer Mannschaft?
Do you play for a team?
Ja, ich spiele Fußball für die Schulmannschaft.
Yes, I play football for the school team.

Wo und wann spielst
du Basketball?
Where and when do you
play basketball?
Wir spielen ab und zu im
Freizeitzentrum Basketball.
We play basketball from time
to time at the leisure centre.

Wie oft spielst du Fußball?
How often do you play football?
Einmal in der Woche gehe ich zum
Training, und dann am Samstag spielen
wir hier in der Schule.
I go training once a week and then on
Saturdays we play here at school.

Vocabulary

spielen	- to play	das Stadion	- stadium
gewinnen	- to win	das Sportzentrum	- sports centre
Fußball	- football	im Sportzentrum	- at the sports centre
Rugby	- rugby	auf dem Sportplatz	- on the sports field
Tennis	- tennis	in der Schule	- at school
Tischtennis	- table tennis	im Jugendzentrum/	
Federball/Badminton	- badminton	im Jugendclub	} - at the youth club
Netzball	- netball	im Park	- in the park
Hockey	- hockey	im Freizeitzentrum	- at the leisure centre
Schach	- chess	im Hallenbad	- at the swimming baths
Karten	- cards	im Freibad	- at the open air swimming pool
Radfahren	- cycling	mit Freunden	- with friends
Windsurfen	- windsurfing	allein	- alone
Leichtathletik	- athletics	in einer Mannschaft	- for a team
das Musikinstrument	- musical instrument	in einer Band	- in a band
Gitarre	- guitar	in einem Orchester	- in an orchestra
Klavier	- piano	in einem Chor singen	- to sing in a choir
Geige	- violin	das Mitglied	- member
Trompete	- trumpet	der Verein/der Klub	- club
Blockflöte	- recorder	bist du Mitglied	} Are you a
Flöte	- flute	eines Klubs	} member of a club?
Schlagzeug	- drums		

Higher

Kannst du das Spiel "rounders" erklären?
Can you explain the game of rounders?
Es gibt zwei Mannschaften. Man muss den Ball schlagen und eine Runde laufen,
um einen Punkt zu kriegen. Die Mannschaft mit den meisten Punkten gewinnt.
There are two teams. You have to hit the ball, and run round without stopping
in order to score a point. The team with the most points wins.

Deiner Meinung nach, sollte
man mehr Sport in der Schule treiben?
In your opinion, ought we to play more
sport in school?
Ich glaube, dass wir mehr Sport treiben
sollten. Das ist sehr wichtig für die
Gesundheit. Heutzutage verbringt man zu
viel Zeit vor dem Fernseher oder vor dem
Computer.
I think we ought to play more sport. It is
very important for one's health. People
spend too much time these days in
front of the TV or computer.

Seit wann spielst du Basketball?
How long have you been playing
basketball?
Ich spiele seit fünf Jahren Basketball,
seitdem ich in dieser Schule bin.
I've been playing basketball for
5 years, since I've been at
this school.

Grammar

Adverbs of Time and Word Order

The following are all time phrases, some of which you may find useful when discussing
free time activities:

oft	-	often
manchmal	-	sometimes
jeden Tag	-	every day
jeden Mittwoch	-	every Wednesday
am Wochenende	-	at the weekend
am Dienstag/dienstags	-	on Tuesdays
am Vormittag	-	in the morning
am Nachmittag	-	in the afternoon
am Abend	-	in the evening
ab und zu	-	occasionally
einmal, zweimal { in der Woche }	-	once, twice a week
{ im Monat }	-	a month

e.g. am Wochenende spiele ich Tennis
heute abend spielen wir Hockey
ich spiele ab und zu Volleyball
Wir gehen zweimal in der Woche zum Training

 Remember: that in the above examples the time phrase appears either BEFORE or AFTER the verb.
When the sentence begins with a time phrase the subject and verb are inverted (change places)
SO THAT THE VERB ALWAYS REMAINS THE SECOND IDEA IN THE SENTENCE.

Foundation

Was machst du nicht gern?
What do you not enjoy doing?
Ich sehe nicht gern Sport im Fernsehen.
I don't enjoy watching
sport on TV.

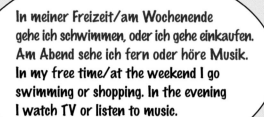

Was machst du in deiner
Freizeit/am Wochenende/am Abend?
What do you do in your free time/at
the weekend/in the evening?

Was machst du gern zu
Hause in deiner Freizeit?
What do you enjoy doing
at home in your free time?
Ich spiele gern Computerspiele und
ich lese gern Romane.
I enjoy playing on the computer
and I like reading novels.

In meiner Freizeit/am Wochenende
gehe ich schwimmen, oder ich gehe einkaufen.
Am Abend sehe ich fern oder höre Musik.
In my free time/at the weekend I go
swimming or shopping. In the evening
I watch TV or listen to music.

Gehst du oft ins Kino?
Do you go to the cinema often?
Ich gehe normalerweise einmal im Monat ins Kino.
I normally go to the cinema once a month.

Gehst du oft mit deinen Freunden aus?
Do you go out often with your friends?
Ja, am Wochenende gehen wir oft in die
Disco oder auf eine Party.
Yes, at the weekend we often go to the
disco or to a party.

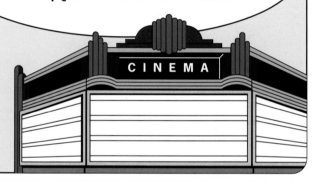

Vocabulary

einkaufen gehen	-	to go shopping		im Fernsehen	-	on TV
schwimmen gehen	-	to go swimming		die Stereoanlage	-	stereo system
reiten	-	to go horse riding		der CD Spieler	-	cd player
Schlittschuh laufen	-	ice skating		Musik hören	-	to listen to music
Rollschuh laufen	-	rollerskating		die Sendung	-	TV programme
Ski laufen/fahren	-	to go skiing		die Komödie	-	comedy
joggen	-	to go jogging		die Seifenoper	-	soap opera
Rad fahren	-	to go cycling		die Nachrichten	-	news
spazieren gehen	-	to go for a walk		der Dokumentarfilm	-	documentary
wandern	-	to walk, hike		lesen	-	to read
angeln	-	to go fishing		der Roman	-	novel
fotografieren	-	to take photographs		der Krimi	-	detective novel
kegeln	-	to go bowling		die Liebesgeschichte	-	love story
tanzen	-	to dance		sammeln	-	to collect
in die Stadt gehen	-	to go into town		die Sammlung	-	collection
ins Kino gehen	-	to go to the cinema		interessant	-	interesting
das Hallenbad	-	swimming pool		lustig	-	amusing, funny
das Freibad	-	outdoor swimming pool		toll		
die Disco	-	disco		prima	} -	great
die Party	-	party		klasse		
ausgehen	-	to go out		langweilig	-	boring
fernsehen	-	to watch TV		ich interessiere mich für	-	I am interested in

Higher

Was hast du neulich im Kino gesehen? Wie war der Film?

What have you seen at the cinema recently? What did you think of the film?

Ich habe letzte Woche "Titanic" gesehen. Es handelt sich um den Untergang des berühmten Schiffs, aber es ist auch eine Liebesgeschichte, und ich fand den Film ganz traurig am Ende. Die Schauspieler Leonardo di Caprio und Kate Winslett waren echt gut.

Last week I saw "Titanic". It is about the sinking of the famous ship, but it is also a love story, and I thought it was very sad at the end. The actors Leonardo di Caprio and Kate Winslett were really good.

Was machst du nächstes Wochenende?

What are you going to do next weekend?

Nächsten Samstag fahre ich mit meiner Freundin nach London. Wir wollen Kleider kaufen, und am Abend wollen wir, uns ein Musical an sehen. Am Sonntag besuche ich meine Tante in Stafford.

Next weekend I'm going to London with my friend. We want to buy some clothes, and we hope to see a musical in the evening. On Sunday I'm going to see my aunt in Stafford.

Grammar

Strong Verbs in the Present Tense

The following verbs all have a vowel change in the DU and ER/SIE/ES forms in the present tense :

fahren - to go, travel	sehen - to see	lesen - to read
ich fahre	ich sehe	ich lese
du fährst	du siehst	du liest
er/sie/es fährt	er/sie/es sieht	er/sie/es liest
wir fahren	wir sehen	wir lesen
ihr fahrt	ihr seht	ihr lest
Sie fahren	Sie sehen	Sie lesen
sie fahren	sie sehen	sie lesen

Use of the Present Tense in German to Express the Future

In German the present tense can be used to expess what one is going to do in the future

e.g. Was machst du nächstes Wochenende/heute abend?

What are you going to do next weekend/this evening?

Nächstes Wochenende spiele ich Hockey/heute abend sehe ich fern.

Next weekend I AM GOING TO play hockey/this evening I AM GOING TO watch TV.

Mini Test

Talk for two minutes in German about your hobbies and interests. Include details such as where? how often? with whom? When you are happy with your speech, record it onto tape.

Foundation

Hast du Lust, heute Abend auszugehen?
Would you like to go out tonight?
Es tut mir Leid, heute abend kann ich nicht.
I'm sorry, I can't make it tonight.

Um wie viel Uhr? At what time?
Um Viertel vor acht. At a quarter to eight.
Gut. Bis dann! Good. See you then!

Hast du Samstag Abend etwas vor?
Have you got something planned for Saturday evening?
Nein, ich habe nichts vor.
No, I've got nothing planned.

Wo treffen wir uns?
Vor dem Kino?
Where shall we meet?
Outside the cinema?
Nein, ich hole dich ab.
No, I'll come and pick you up.

Willst du mit mir ins Kino gehen?
Would you like to go to the cinema with me?
Ja, was läuft?
Yes, what's on?

Was kostet der Eintritt?
What does it cost to go in?
Das kostet fünf Euros.
It costs 5 Euros.

Es läuft der neue James Bond Film.
The new James Bond film.
Toll ! Abenteuerfilme sehe ich sehr gern.
Great ! I really like adventure films.

Wann ist der Film zu Ende?
What time does the film end?
Um zweiundzwanzig Uhr.
At 10.00pm.

Wann beginnt der Film?
When does the film start?
Die letzte Vorstellung beginnt um zwanzig Uhr zehn.
The last performance begins at 8.10 p.m.

HOLLYWOOD
MOVIES

Vocabulary

sich treffen	to meet	der Film ist frei ab 16	you have to be 16 to see this film
hast du Lust?	do you want to?	das Theater	theatre
gute Idee	good idea	ins Theater gehen	to go to the theatre
ich würde gern	I would like to	das Theaterstück	play
mir ist egal	I don't mind	die Vorstellung	performance
es tut mir Leid	I'm sorry	das Konzert	concert
ich kann nicht	I can't	ins Konzert gehen	to go to a concert
leider	unfortunately	die (Eintritts) Karte	ticket
schade	what a shame	der Eintritt	entry, admission
etwas vorhaben	to have something planned	einladen	to invite
was läuft?	what's on?	anrufen / telefonieren	to telephone
romantische Filme	romantic films		
der Abenteuerfilm	adventure film		
der Actionfilm	action film	sich treffen	to meet
der Western	western	abholen	to pick up
der Sciencefictionfilm	science fiction film	besorgen	to obtain (tickets etc)
der Trickfilm	cartoon, animated film	ausverkauft	sold out
der Gruselfilm / der Horrorfilm	horror film	abgemacht	agreed
		in Ordnung	OK, fine
der Schauspieler	actor	bis dann	see you then

Higher

Hast du Lust, nächstes Wochenende mit mir kegeln zu gehen?
Would you like to go bowling with me next weekend?
Ich würde lieber ins Theater gehen, um das Shakespeare Theaterstück "Viel Lärm Um Nichts" zu sehen.
I would rather go to the theatre, to see the Shakespeare play, "Much Ado About Nothing"

Gut. Wie wäre es mit Freitagabend?
Fine. How about Friday evening?
Freitag habe ich schon etwas vor; Samstagabend wäre besser.
I've already got something on on Friday. Saturday evening would be better.
In Ordnung. Ich werde anrufen, um zu sehen, ob es noch Karten gibt.
OK. I shall telephone to see if there are still tickets available.

Grammar

Prepositions Governing the Dative or the Accusative

The prepositions listed below are followed by the **DATIVE** or the **ACCUSATIVE** depending on whether there is movement involved or not :-

in	-	in	zwischen	-	between
an	-	at, on	unter	-	under
auf	-	at, on	über	-	over, above
vor	-	in front of	neben	-	next to, near
hinter	-	behind			

e.g. ich fahre in die Stadt (accusative)
I'm going INTO town (movement involved)
treffen wir uns in der Stadt (dative)
let's meet IN town (already there, no movement involved)

die Karten sind auf dem Tisch (dative)
the tickets are on the table (no movement involved)
ich habe die Karten auf den Tisch gelegt (accusative)
I put the tickets on the table (movement involved)

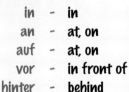

Prepositions followed by the **DATIVE** indicate **WHERE SOMETHING IS.**
Prepositions followed by the **ACCUSATIVE** indicate **MOVEMENT.**

Note also these contracted forms :

an dem	-	**am**	an das	-	**ans**
in dem	-	**im**	in das	-	**ins**

Mini Test

1. Practise inviting someone out; suggest different venues, times and meeting places.
2. Practise accepting and refusing invitations, always giving a reason when you refuse!

Foundation

Wann stehst du an Wochentagen/am Wochenende auf?
What time do you get up on weekdays/at the weekend?
An Wochentagen stehe ich um Viertel vor sieben auf und am
Wochenende stehe ich normalerweise um neun Uhr auf.
On weekdays I get up at a quarter to seven, and at the weekend
I normally get up about nine o' clock.

Um wie viel Uhr gehst du ins Bett?
What time do you go to bed?
Ich gehe normalerweise um halb elf
ins Bett, aber dann lese ich.
I normally go to bed at half past ten,
but then I read.

Was machst du dann?
What do you do then?
Ich wasche mich/dusche mich und ziehe mich an.
I have a wash/shower and get dressed.

Was machst du am Abend?
What do you do in the evening?
Ich muss zuerst meine Hausaufgaben
machen. Wir essen um sechs zu Abend,
und dann sehe ich ein bisschen fern.
I have to do my homework first.
We eat our evening meal at six o'clock
and then I watch a bit of TV.

Wann isst du Frühstück?
What time do you have breakfast?
An Wochentagen frühstücke ich um zwanzig nach sieben.
On weekdays I have breakfast at twenty past seven.

Wann gehst du zur Schule?
What time do you go to school?
Ich verlasse das Haus um zehn vor acht.
I leave the house at ten to eight.

Und wann kommst du nach Hause?
And what time do you get home?
Ich komme um Viertel nach vier wieder nach Hause.
I get home at a quarter past four.

Vocabulary

auf/wachen	-	to wake up
auf/stehen	-	to get up
sich duschen	-	to have a shower
sich waschen	-	to have a wash
sich an/ziehen	-	to get dressed
sich aus/ziehen	-	to get undressed
sich um/ziehen	-	to get changed
sich die Zähne putzen	-	to clean your teeth
sich entspannen	-	to rest, relax, unwind
ins Bett gehen	-	to go to bed
ein/schlafen	-	to fall asleep, go to sleep

aus/schlafen	-	to have a good sleep
schlafen	-	to sleep
früh	-	early
spät	-	late
später	-	later
zuerst	-	first of all
dann	-	then
nachher	-	afterwards
bevor + verb	-	before
vor + noun	-	before
e.g. bevor ich in die Schule gehe	-	before I go to school
vor dem Frühstück	-	before breakfast
nach + noun	-	after
nachdem + verb	-	after
e.g. nach dem Frühstück	-	after breakfast
nachdem ich das Haus verlasse	-	after I leave the house

Higher

Beschreib deine tägliche Routine.
Describe your daily routine.
In der Woche stehe ich ziemlich früh auf. Ich gehe ins Badezimmer, dusche mich und ziehe mich schnell an ...
During the week I get up quite early. I go into the bathroom, have a shower and then quickly get dressed ...

Hast du lieber Wochentage oder Wochenenden? Warum?
Do you prefer weekdays or the weekend? Why?
Ich habe Wochenenden lieber; ich kann mich gut entspannen.
I prefer weekends; I can really relax/unwind.

Um wie viel Uhr bist du gestern aufgestanden?
What time did you get up yesterday?
Ich bin gestern um sieben Uhr aufgestanden.
Ich habe mich geduscht und mich schnell angezogen ...
Yesterday I got up at seven. I had a shower and quickly got dressed ...

Und wie ist das am Wochenende anders?
And how does that differ at the weekend?
Am Wochenende schlafe ich gut aus, und stehe später auf.
At the weekend I have a good sleep, and get up later.

Grammar

Reflexive Verbs in the Present Tense

The topic "Daily routine" contains a number of common REFLEXIVE VERBS :
sich waschen (to have a wash), sich anziehen (to get dressed).
"SICH" indicates that the verb is reflexive i.e. something you do to or for yourself e.g. sich waschen - to wash oneself as opposed to das Auto waschen - to wash the car.
The reflexive pronoun SICH will change to agree with the subject of the verb as follows :

SICH WASCHEN

ich wasche mich	- I have a wash		wir waschen uns	- we have a wash
du wäscht dich	- you have a wash		ihr wascht euch	- you have a wash
er/sie/es wäscht sich	- he/she has a wash		Sie/sie waschen sich	- you/they have a wash

Reflexive verbs in German can be weak or strong; you can see that waschen is a STRONG verb (change of vowel sound in the DU and ER/SIE/ES forms)

Reflexive Verbs in the Perfect Tense

All reflexive verbs take the auxiliary verb HABEN in the perfect tense. Note word order :

ich habe mich gewaschen - I had a wash
ich habe mich angezogen - I got dressed (reflexive and separable)

Mini Test

1. Say 10 things about your daily routine, using a variety of verbs and times.
2. Now change that information for your weekend routine.

Foundation

In was für einem Haus wohnst du?
What kind of a house do you live in?
Ich wohne in einem modernen Doppelhaus.
I live in a modern semi-detached house.

Wie viele Zimmer gibt es?
How many rooms are there?
Es gibt acht Zimmer - drei Schlafzimmer,
ein Badezimmer, ein Wohnzimmer, ein Eßzimmer,
eine Küche und ein Arbeitszimmer.
**There are 8 rooms - 3 bedrooms, a bathroom,
a living room, a dining room, a kitchen
and a study.**

Teilst du dein Zimmer?
Do you share a room?
Ja, ich teile mit meinem
Bruder/meiner Schwester.
Nein, ich habe mein eigenes Zimmer.
**Yes, I share with my brother/sister.
No, I have my own room.**

Habt ihr einen Garten/eine Garage?
Do you have a garden/garage?
Ja, beides Wir haben zwei Gärten - einer vor und einer hinter
dem Haus, und neben dem Haus haben wir eine Garage.
**Yes, both. We have 2 gardens - one in front and one behind
the house, and next to the house we have a garage.**

Kannst du dein Zimmer beschreiben?
Can you describe your bedroom?
Mein Schlafzimmer ist ganz klein. Es gibt ein Bett, einen Kleiderschrank,
eine Kommode und viele Poster an der Wand. Die Wände sind blau
tapeziert, und ich habe einen dunkelblauen Teppich.
**My bedroom is really small. There is a bed, a wardrobe, a chest
of drawers and lots of posters on the wall. The walls have
blue wallpaper and I have a dark blue carpet.**

Vuolary

das Einfamilienhaus	detached house
das Doppelhaus	semi-detached house
das Reihenhaus	terraced house
die Wohnung	flat
der Bauernhof	farm
der Bungalow	bungalow
der Keller	cellar
der Dachboden	attic
der Garten	garden
die Garage	garage
die Blumen	flowers
die Bäume	trees
der Rasen	lawn
der Wintergarten	conservatory
die Terrasse	terrace, patio
der Flur	hall
das Wohnzimmer	living room
das Eßzimmer	dining room
das Arbeitszimmer	study
das Schlafzimmer	bedroom
das Badezimmer	bathroom
die Küche	kitchen
die Dusche	shower
die Treppe	stairs

das WC	toilet
die Waschküche	utility room
das Zimmer	room
der Fernseher	television
das Videogerät	video machine
der Videorekorder	video recorder
das Bett	bed
der Kleiderschrank	wardrobe
die Kommode	chest of drawers
der Tisch	table
der Nachttisch	bedside table
der Stuhl	chair
der Sessel	armchair
das Sofa	sofa
das Regal	shelf
der Teppich	carpet
die Vorhänge	curtains
die Wand	(inside) wall
an der Wand	on the wall
auf dem Boden	on the floor
ordentlich	tidy
unordentlich	untidy
teilen	to share

Higher

Seit wann wohnst du in deinem Haus?
How long have you been living in your house?
Ich wohne seit drei Jahren dort.
I have been living there for three years.

Gefällt dir dein Zimmer?
Do you like your room?
Mein Schlafzimmer gefällt mir ziemlich gut;
die Farben habe ich selber ausgewählt, aber
die Möbel sind ein bisschen altmodisch.
I quite like my bedroom; I chose the
colours myself, but the furniture is
a bit old-fashioned.

Beschreib dein Traumhaus.
Describe your ideal home.
Mein Traumhaus würde sehr groß sein,
mit wenigstens zwanzig Zimmern,
einem Hallenbad und einer Sauna.
My dream house would be very big,
with at least 20 rooms, an indoor
swimming pool and a sauna.

Wie würdest du dein Zimmer verändern?
How would you change your room?
Ich würde neue Möbel kaufen und neue
Vorhänge aussuchen.
I would buy new furniture and
choose new curtains.

Grammar

Question Words

wann	-	when?	wie lange	- how long?
wo	-	where?	wie viel	- how many?
wer	-	who?	welche/r/s	- which?
was	-	what?	warum	- why?
was für	-	what kind of?	seit wann	- for how long?
wie	-	how?		

After a question word, remember to invert subject and verb :

e.g. wo wohnst du? where do you live?
wie viele Zimmer hat dein Haus? How many rooms does your house have?

Sometimes you can simply invert the subject and verb to change a statement into a question :

e.g. du teilst dein Zimmer mit deiner Schwester
you share your room with your sister
teilst du dein Zimmer?
do you share your room ?

 Remember: that you have to be able to ask,
as well as answer questions at GCSE.

Use of SEIT

To express the idea that something has been happening for a certain length of time AND IS STILL HAPPENING,
SEIT + present tense is used :

e.g. seit wann wohnst du in Northampton?
ich wohne seit drei Jahren hier - I have been living here for 3 years

N.B. Seit is a preposition governing the dative - drei Jahre (plural) seit 3 Jahren (dative plural)

Mini Test

1. Say as much as you can in German about your house and bedroom. Record yourself onto tape.
2. Describe your ideal home in German.
3. Practise asking questions in German, using as many different question words as possible.

Foundation

Sparst du etwas? Wofür?
Do you save anything? What for?
Ja, ich spare für die Ferien und für Geschenke.
Yes, I'm saving up for the holidays and for presents.

Bekommst du Taschengeld?
Do you get pocket money?
Wie viel?
How much?
Ich bekomme fünf Pfund pro
Woche von meinen Eltern.
I get £5 a week from my parents.

Was machst du mit deinem Geld?
What do you do with your money?
Ich kaufe Kleider und CDs.
I buy clothes and CDs.

Musst du dafür im Haushalt helfen?
Do you have to help with the housework for it?
Ja, ich muss mein Zimmer aufräumen, den Tisch
decken und mit dem Hund spazierengehen.
**Yes, I have to tidy my room, set the
table and walk the dog.**

Wie viel verdienst du?
Wie ist deine Arbeitszeit?
How much do you earn?
What hours do you work?
Ich verdiene zwanzig Pfund pro Tag;
ich arbeite samstags von neun Uhr
bis halb sechs.
**I earn £20 a day; I work Saturdays
from 9a.m. to 5.30 p.m.**

Wie verdienst du dein Geld?
Hast du einen Job?
How do you earn your money?
Do you have a part-time job?
Samstags arbeite ich in einem Supermarkt, und
ab und zu mache ich Babysitten.
**On Saturdays I work in a supermarket and
I do some babysitting from time to time.**

Vocabulary

im Haushalt helfen	- to help with the housework		einkaufen gehen	- to go shopping
die Hausarbeit	- housework		das Auto waschen	- to wash the car
ab/waschen	} - to wash up		das Taschengeld	- pocket money
ab/spülen			bekommen	- to receive
ab/trocknen	- to dry the dishes		verdienen	- to earn
auf/räumen	- to tidy up		Geld aus/geben	- to spend money
kochen	- to cook		kaufen	- to buy
das Abendessen vor/bereiten	- to prepare the evening meal		sparen	- to save
die Wäsche machen	- to do the washing		das Pfund	- £1
bügeln	- to iron		pro Tag/Woche/Monat	- per day/week/month
den Tisch decken	- to set the table		arbeiten	- to work
mit dem Hund spazierengehen	- to walk the dog		in einem Supermarkt	- in a supermarket
die Betten machen	- to make the beds		in einem Geschäft	- in a shop
staub/saugen	- to hoover, vacuum clean		bei einem Friseur	- at a hairdresser's
putzen	- to clean		an der Kasse	- at the cash desk
im Garten arbeiten	- to do the gardening		Zeitungen austragen	- to deliver newspapers
den Rasen mähen	- to mow the lawn		Babysitten machen	- to babysit

Higher

Was hast du letzte Woche
mit deinem Taschengeld gemacht?
**What did you do with your pocket
money last week?**
Ich habe eine neue Hose gekauft
und ich habe zehn Pfund in mein
Bankkonto eingezahlt.
**I bought a new pair of trousers
and I put £10 in the bank.**

Was hast du gestern gemacht,
um deinen Eltern im Haushalt zu helfen?
**What did you do yesterday to help your parents
around the house?**
Ich habe die Betten gemacht und mein Zimmer
aufgeräumt. Ich habe auch meinem Bruder
geholfen, das Abendessen vorzubereiten.
**I made the beds and tidied my room.
I also helped my brother prepare
the evening meal.**

Musst du mehr als deine Schwester/dein Bruder im Haushalt helfen?
Do you have to help out more than your sister/brother at home?
Nein, das haben unsere Eltern ganz fair aufgeteilt. Ich helfe in der Küche
und mein Bruder hilft meiner Mutter im Garten.
**No, my parents have divided it quite fairly. I help in the kitchen and my
brother helps my mother in the garden.**

Grammar

Separable Verbs

In the present tense, the first part of the separable verb, **THE SEPARABLE PREFIX**, e.g. ab, auf, an etc, goes to the **END** of the clause or sentence :

e.g. ich spüle jeden Abend <u>ab</u> - I wash up every evening
     ich räume nicht gern mein Zimmer <u>auf</u> - I don't like tidying my room

When used with a **MODAL** verb, the separable prefix again joins back together with the verb in the infinitive at the end of the sentence/clause :

e.g. ich muss mein Zimmer <u>auf</u>räumen - I have to tidy my room
     er kann jetzt <u>ab</u>trocknen - he can dry the dishes now

In the **PERFECT** tense, the separable prefix once again joins with the **PAST PARTICIPLE** at the end of the sentence/clause :

e.g. ich habe mein Zimmer <u>auf</u>geräumt - I (have) tidied, did tidy my room
     ich habe das Abendessen <u>vor</u>bereitet - I (have) prepared, did prepare the evening meal.

Similarly, when separable verbs are used with verbs requiring **ZU + INFINITIVE**, the separable verb appears in the infinitive at the end of the sentence/clause with the **ZU BETWEEN** the separable prefix and the verb, and **NOT PRECEDING THE INFINITIVE AS WITH INSEPARABLE VERBS** :

e.g. ich habe meinem Bruder geholfen, das Abendessen vor<u>ZU</u>bereiten.
     I helped my brother prepare the evening meal.

Mini Test

1. Describe in German what each member of the family does to help with the household chores.
2. Make a list in German of what you have spent your money on in the last month.
3. Explain how you earn your (pocket) money.

Foundation

Kannst du einen typischen Schultag beschreiben?
Can you describe a typical school day?
Die erste Stunde beginnt um neun Uhr. Die Pause ist um Viertel nach zehn und dauert zwanzig Minuten. Wir essen um eins zu Mittag ...
The first lesson starts at 9am. Break is at 10.15 and lasts 20 minutes. We have lunch at 1 o'clock ...

Wie ist deine Schule?
What is your school like?
Meine Schule ist eine Gesamtschule und ist groß und modern. Es gibt zwölf hundert Schüler und siebzig Lehrer.
My school is a comprehensive and is big and modern. There are 1200 pupils and 70 teachers.

Trägst du eine Schuluniform?
Do you wear a school uniform?
Ja, wir tragen einen blauen Pullover, einen grauen Rock oder eine graue Hose und ein weißes Hemd.
Yes, we wear a blue pullover, a grey skirt or trousers and a white shirt.

Wann beginnt die Schule?
What time does school start?
Die Schule beginnt um Viertel vor neun, und ist um zwanzig vor vier aus.
School starts at 8.45 and finishes at 3.40 pm.

Welche Fächer hast du?
Which subjects are you studying?
Ich lerne Mathe, Englisch, Deutsch und sechs weitere Fächer.
I'm taking maths, English, German and 6 other subjects.

Was ist dein Lieblingsfach?
What is your favourite subject?
Mein Lieblingsfach ist Mathe, weil es nützlich ist.
My favourite subject is maths, because it is useful.

Vocabulary

eine Schule besuchen	-	to go to, attend school	Sozialwissenschaften	-	social sciences
die Gesamtschule	-	comprehensive school	Hausaufgaben	-	homework
die Hauptschule	-	secondary modern school	die Note	-	mark
die Realschule	-	type of secondary school	die Prüfung	-	exam
das Gymnasium	-	grammar school	die Stunde	-	lesson
das Fach	-	school subject	der Lehrer/die -in	-	teacher (m/f)
das Wahlfach	-	option	der Schüler/die -in	-	pupil (m/f)
Mathe(matik)	-	maths	die Pause	-	break
Englisch	-	English	die Mittagspause	-	lunch hour
Deutsch	-	German	der Stundenplan	-	timetable
Französisch	-	French	die Schuluniform	-	school uniform
Naturwissenschaft	-	science	interessant	-	interesting
Biologie	-	biology	leicht	-	easy
Chemie	-	chemistry	Spaß machen	-	to be fun
Physik	-	physics	es macht Spaß	-	it is fun
Geschichte	-	history	langweilig	-	boring
Geographie/Erdkunde	-	geography	schwierig	-	difficult
Informatik	-	IT	nützlich	-	useful
Werken	-	design technology	bequem	-	comfortable
Sport	-	PE, sport	praktisch	-	practical
Religion	-	religious education	wichtig	-	important
Kunst	-	art	streng	-	strict
Technik	-	technology	das Zeugnis	-	report
Hauswirtschaft (slehre)	-	home economics			

Higher

Was hast du gestern in der Schule gemacht?
What did you do in school yesterday?
Gestern hatte ich zuerst eine Doppelstunde Kunst. Nach der Pause hatte ich Mathe und Deutsch. In der Mittagspause habe ich Hockey gespielt und am Nachmittag habe ich in der Musikstunde Mozart gehört.
First of all yesterday I had a double lesson of art. After break I had maths and German. At lunchtime I played hockey and in the afternoon I listened to Mozart during my music lesson.

Deiner Meinung nach, was ist wichtiger, Mathe oder Erdkunde?
In your opinion which is more important, maths or geography?
Ich finde Mathe wichtiger als Erdkunde, aber für mich sind Fremdsprachen die wichtigsten Fächer, weil ich später im Ausland arbeiten möchte.
I think that maths is more important than geography, but for me, foreign languages are the most important subjects, because I would like to work abroad.

Grammar

Comparative and Superlative of Adjectives

In English the comparative and superlative of adjectives works in the following way :

ADJECTIVE	COMPARATIVE	SUPERLATIVE
small	smaller	smallest
important	more important	most important

In German, adjectives take "er" in the comparative and "(e)st" in the superlative (plus the adjective ending where appropriate). Many single syllable adjectives also take an umlaut where appropriate:

(important)	wichtig	wichtiger	der/die/das wichtigste
(interesting)	interessant	interessanter	der/die/das interessanteste
(short)	kurz	kürzer	der/die/das kürzeste
(old)	alt	älter	der/die/das älteste
(small)	klein	kleiner	der/die/das kleinste

e.g. Deutsch ist interessanter als Mathe - **German is more interesting than maths**
Meiner Meinung nach ist Englisch das wichtigste Fach - **in my opinion English is the most important subject.**

Note the irregular:

(good)	gut	besser	der/die/das beste
(big, tall)	groß	größer	der/die/das größte
(tall)	hoch	höher	der/die/das höchste
(near)	nah	näher	der/die/das nächste

Comparatives and superlatives require an adjective ending, as any adjective does, according to gender and case:
e.g. Ich bekomme immer besser<u>e</u> Noten in Biologie als in Physik.
I always get better marks in biology than in physics.

Mini Test

1. Prepare a speech in German about your school. Mention the subjects you do, your opinion of them, and describe the school itself and some of your teachers.

Foundation

> Was wirst du nächstes Jahr/nächsten September machen?
> **What are you going to do next year/next September?**
> Ich werde hier an der Schule bleiben und weiterlernen/Ich werde mir eine Stelle suchen.
> **I'm going to stay on at school and continue my studies/I'm going to look for a job.**

> Welche Fächer wirst du wählen?
> **Which subjects are you going to study?**
> Ich werde Biologie, Erdkunde und Mathe studieren.
> **I'm going to study biology, geography and maths.**

> Was möchtest du später als Beruf machen?
> **What job/career would you like to pursue?**
> Ich möchte/ich werde Ingenieur(in) sein/werden.
> **I would like/I am going to be/become an engineer.**

The female form of jobs and professions is formed by adding '-in' to the male form, and changing the gender to 'die'. Exceptions to this rule are also shown below.

Vocabulary

der Arzt/die Ärztin	-	doctor
der Zahnarzt/die -ärztin	-	dentist
der Tierarzt/die -ärztin	-	vet
der Krankenpfleger } die Krankenschwester }	-	nurse
der Apotheker/die -in	-	chemist,pharmacist
der Mechaniker/die -in	-	mechanic
der Ingenieur/die -in	-	engineer
der Bauarbeiter/die -in	-	builder
der Klempner/die -in	-	plumber
der Elektriker/die -in	-	electrician
der Kellner/die -in	-	waiter/waitress
der Bäcker/die -in	-	baker
der Fleischer/die -in } der Metzger/die -in }	-	butcher
der Koch/die Köchin	-	chef
der Verkäufer/die -in	-	sales assistant
der LKW-Fahrer/die -in	-	lorry driver
der Briefträger/die -in	-	postman/womam
der Sekretär/die -in	-	secretary
der Polizist/die -in	-	policeman/woman
der Feuerwehrmann/die-frau	-	firefighter
der Friseur/die Friseuse	-	hairdresser
der Kaufmann/die-frau	-	businessman/woman, trader
der Programmierer/die-in	-	computer programmer
der Rechtsanwalt/die-anwältin	-	lawyer
der Journalist/die-in	-	journalist
der Bauer/die Bäuerin	-	farmer

der Beamte/die Beamtin	-	official, civil servant
der/die Angestellte	-	employee, clerk
der Geschäftsmann } die -frau }	-	businessman/woman
der Arbeitgeber/die -in	-	employer
die Arbeit	-	work
die Stelle	-	job, position
der Arbeiter/die -in	-	worker
in einer Bank	-	in a bank
in einem Büro	-	in an office
in einer Fabrik	-	in a factory
bei einer Firma	-	for a firm, company
im Freien	-	outdoors
im Ausland	-	abroad
mit anderen Leuten	-	with other people
mit Kindern	-	with children
allein	-	alone
berufstätig	-	employed
arbeitslos	-	unemployed
selbstständig	-	self-employed, independent
der Lehrling	-	apprentice
das Abitur	-	German equivalent to A Level qualification
der Ausbildungsplatz	-	training vacancy
das Arbeitsamt	-	job centre
die Berufsberatung	-	careers guidance
das Gehalt	-	salary

Higher

> Was sind deine Zukunftspläne/Hoffnungen für die Zukunft?
> What are your future plans/hopes for the future?
> Ich werde mein Abitur machen und dann auf die Uni gehen.
> Dann habe ich vor, im Ausland zu arbeiten. Ich hoffe,
> irgendwann zu heiraten und Kinder zu haben.
> I shall do my A levels and then go to university.
> Then I intend to work abroad. At some point
> I hope to marry and have children.

Grammar

The Future Tense

We have already seen how the present tense can be used in German to express the future (see p.15).
The FUTURE tense in German is formed by using the verb WERDEN + INFINITIVE

e.g. Ich werde mit sechzehn die Schule verlassen - I'm going to leave school at 16
Er wird eine Stelle finden - he is going to find a job
Wir werden weiterstudieren - we are going to continue studying.

WERDEN on its own means "to become". Used together with an infinitive it expresses the future tense in German.

WERDEN

ich werde
du wirst
er/sie/es wird
wir werden
ihr werdet
Sie/sie werden

Verbs Used With ZU + Infinitive

Most verbs in German, when used with an infinitive, require zu in front of the infinitive.
e..g. Ich hoffe, im Ausland zu arbeiten - I hope to work abroad
Sie hat beschlossen, eine Stelle zu suchen - she has decided to look for a job

Note the position of zu with a separable verb in the infinitive :
Er hat vor, in der Oberstufe weiterzustudieren - he intends to continue studying in the Sixth form.

Mini Test

Record yourself on tape talking about your future. What are your plans for:

next September

in 2 years time

in 10 years time ?

Foundation

You may be expected to answer questions in German in an interview situation as part of your oral examination. At Foundation level, this may involve talking about yourself, personal details and qualities (pages 8-9), your interests (pages 12-15), and possibly your education (pages 24-25). You may also be asked some questions about your work experience, as shown below:

Können Sie Ihren Arbeitstag beschreiben?
Can you describe your working day?
Ich habe um neun Uhr angefangen. Wir hatten um elf Uhr eine Kaffeepause, und um eins habe ich in der Kantine gegessen. Ich habe das Büro um fünf Uhr verlassen.
I started at 9 am. We had a coffee break at 11 am and I ate my lunch in the canteen at 1 o'clock. I left the office at 5pm.

Wo war Ihr Arbeitspraktikum?
Where did you do your work experience?
Für mein Arbeitspraktikum habe ich in einem Büro gearbeitet.
I worked in an office for my work experience.

Wie war Ihr Arbeitspraktikum?
How was your work experience?
Die Arbeit hat mir Spaß gemacht.
I enjoyed the work.

Haben Sie Deutsch gesprochen?
Did you speak German?
Ja, ich habe ein bisschen Deutsch am Telefon gesprochen.
Yes, I spoke a little German on the phone.

Was haben Sie gemacht?
What did you do?
Ich habe Dokumente abgelegt und manchmal Briefe getippt. Ich habe auch Telefonanrufe gemacht, und mit Kunden gesprochen.
I did some filing and sometimes typed letters. I also made some telephone calls and spoke to customers.

N.B. As this is a formal interview situation, the "Sie" form of address is used.

Vocabulary

das Arbeitspraktikum	-	work experience	das Internet	-	internet
der Arbeitstag	-	the working day	die Geschäftszeiten	-	hours of business
die Arbeit	-	work	die Kantine	-	canteen
die Aufgabe	-	task	Spaß machen	-	to be fun
der Betrieb	-	business, firm	stressig	-	stressful
Dokumente ablegen	-	to file	die Eigenschaft	-	quality
Telefonanrufe machen	-	to make phone calls	höflich	-	polite
am Telefon	-	on the telephone	hilfreich	-	helpful
Faxe schicken	-	to send faxes	verantwortungsbewusst	-	responsible
der Chef/die Chefin	-	the boss	selbstbewusst	-	self-confident
die Kollegen	-	colleagues	unternehmungslustig	-	outgoing
die Kunden	-	customers	nötig	-	necessary
die Kaffeepause	-	coffee break	die Erfahrung	-	experience
der Computer	-	computer	die Qualifikation	-	qualification
die Diskette	-	disc	die Stellenanzeige	-	job advert
die E-mail	-	e-mail			

Higher

> Warum möchten Sie diese Stelle?
> **Why do you want this job?**
> Ich möchte einen Beruf haben, wo ich viel Kontakt mit anderen Leuten habe. Ich habe die nötige Erfahrung und Qualifikationen, und ich bin verantwortlich und unternehmungslustig.
> **I would like a career where I can have lots of contact with other people. I have the necessary experience and qualifications, and I am responsible and outgoing.**

> Erzählen Sie mir von Ihrem Arbeitspraktikum.
> **Tell me a bit about your work experience.**
> Für zwei Wochen habe ich in einem Büro gearbeitet. Ich habe hauptsächlich mit Computern gearbeitet, und manchmal Kunden besucht. Die Arbeit hat mir gut gefallen.
> **I worked in an office for 2 weeks. I mainly worked with computers, and sometimes visited customers. I enjoyed the work.**

Grammar

The Perfect Tense With HABEN

The PERFECT TENSE is one of the past tenses in German (talking about something that has happened). It is made up of two parts : an AUXILIARY (helping) verb, either HABEN or SEIN and a PAST PARTICIPLE. We will look here at verbs which take HABEN (remind yourself of the verb HABEN - see page 9)

The PAST PARTICIPLE of regular verbs (weak verbs) is formed by removing the EN from the infinitive and adding T, and also adding GE to the front:

e.g. Ich habe Telefonanrufe gemacht - I did make, (have) made telephone calls
      Ich habe Briefe getippt - I (have) typed, did type letters

Note the past participle of arbeiten - gearbeitet - the extra e is inserted, as in the present tense, to make the word easier to say.

Verbs with no ge- in the past participle include verbs that end in -ieren:
Was haben Sie in der Schule studiert? - What did you study at school?

and those with INSEPARABLE prefixes :
be-, ge-, er-, ver-, zer-, emp-, ent-, miss-
e.g. Ich habe zwei Wochen dort verbracht - I spent 2 weeks there
      Wir haben Kunden besucht - we visited customers

There are also many strong and irregular verbs in the perfect tense; you have met some of them here:
e.g. Ich habe in der Kantine gegessen - I ate in the canteen
      Haben Sie Deutsch gesprochen? - Did you speak German?
      These past participles just have to be learnt! (see Verb Table pages 92-93).

Note also the past participle of SEPARABLE verbs:
e.g. Ich habe um neun Uhr angefangen - I started at 9am
      where the ge- comes between the separable prefix and the rest of the verb.

Foundation

Wohnst du gern hier?
Do you like living here?
Ja, ich wohne gern hier; es gibt viele junge Leute.
Yes, I like living here; there are lots of young people.
Nein, ich wohne nicht gern hier; es gibt kein Kino und nur zwei Geschäfte.
No, I don't like living here; there is no cinema and only 2 shops.

Wohnst du in einer Stadt oder in einem Dorf?
Do you live in a town or a village?
Ich wohne in einer Großstadt/ich wohne in einem kleinen Dorf.
I live in a city/I live in a small village.

Wo liegt Milton Keynes?
Where is Milton Keynes?
Milton Keynes liegt in Südostengland, achtzig Kilometer von London entfernt.
Milton Keynes is in the South East of England, 80 km from London.

Was für eine Stadt ist Milton Keynes?
What kind of a town is Milton Keynes?
Milton Keynes ist eine große, moderne Stadt.
Milton Keynes is a large, modern town.

Was kann man in Milton Keynes machen?
What is there to do in Milton Keynes?
Man kann einkaufen gehen, und es gibt viele Sportmöglichkeiten. Am Abend kann man ins Kino gehen oder im Restaurant essen.
You can go shopping, and there are plenty of opportunities for sport. In the evening you can go to the cinema or eat in a restaurant.

Was gibt es in Milton Keynes?
What is there in Milton Keynes?
Es gibt ein Kino, einen Dom und viele Geschäfte.
There is a cinema, a cathedral and lots of shops.

Vocabulary

die Stadt	-	town	der See	-	lake
das Dorf	-	village	das Feld	-	field
die Großstadt	-	city	der Bauernhof	-	farm
die Stadtmitte } das Stadtzentrum	-	town centre	die Einwohner	-	inhabitants
			der Abfall	-	rubbish, litter
auf dem Lande	-	in the countryside	die Kneipe	-	pub
die Landschaft	-	scenery	der Markt	-	market
im Vorort	-	in the suburbs	die Kirche	-	church
am Stadtrand	-	on the edge of town	der Dom	-	cathedral
die Gegend	-	area, region	das Einkaufszentrum	-	shopping centre
liegen } sich befinden	-	to be situated	das Sportzentrum	-	sports centre
			das Freizeitzentrum	-	leisure centre
in der Nähe (von)	-	near (to), nearby	das Krankenhaus	-	hospital
80 km entfernt	-	80 km away, distant	der Park	-	park
besuchen	-	to visit	die Bibliothek	-	library
schmutzig	-	dirty	der Bahnhof	-	railway station
sauber	-	clean	der Busbahnhof	-	bus station
verschmutzt	-	polluted	im Norden/Süden/ Osten/Westen }	-	in the north/south/ east/west
ruhig	-	peaceful			
der Fluss	-	river	in Nordwestengland	-	in North West England
der Wald	-	wood	in Südostengland	-	in South East England

Higher

Was sind die Vorteile und Nachteile, in einer Stadt/auf dem Lande zu wohnen?

What are the advantages and disadvantages of living in a town/in the countryside?

In der Stadt ist immer viel los, aber es gibt auch viel Lärm und viel Verkehr auf der Straße. Auf dem Lande ist es ruhig, aber es kann auch manchmal langweilig sein.

In the town there is always plenty to do, but there is also a lot of noise, and lots of traffic on the roads. It is peaceful in the countryside, but it can also be boring at times.

Würdest du lieber in einer Stadt oder auf dem Lande wohnen? Warum?

Would you prefer to live in a town or in the countryside? Why?

Ich würde lieber in einer Stadt wohnen, weil es viele junge Leute gibt, und man viel unternehmen kann.

I would prefer to live in a town, because there are lots of young people, and there is plenty to do.

Grammar

ES GIBT + Accusative

Es gibt is used in German to express "there is" or "there are". It is always followed by the accusative case:

e.g. Es gibt einen modernen Bahnhof (m) - **there is a modern railway station**
Es gibt eine alte Kirche (f) - **an old church**
Es gibt ein interessantes Museum (nt) - **an interesting museum**
Es gibt viele kleine Geschäfte (pl) - **lot of little shops**

Note that adjectives have the appropriate endings, depending on case (here - accusative), and gender.

Modal Verbs (1)

Modal verbs are most frequently used together with another verb in the infinitive. The second verb goes to the end of the clause or sentence. The six modal verbs in German are:
können (to be able to), müssen (to have to), wollen (to want to), dürfen (to be allowed to), sollen (to be supposed to), mögen (to like).

e.g. In Milton Keynes kann man einkaufen gehen
you can go shopping in Milton Keynes
Manchester soll für Touristen interessant sein
Manchester is supposed to be an interesting place for tourists
Ich mag es hier! - **I like it here!** (often used on its own in the present tense)

All six modal verbs are irregular. Please see Verb Tables page 88 and pages 92-93 for details.
More examples of modal verbs can be found on page 35.

Mini Test

1. How many buildings can you name in German in one minute? Check genders and spelling!
2. Describe your own town/village, listing the facilities available, and using as many adjectives as you can; then check that adjective agreements correspond correctly with gender and case.
3. Draw up 2 lists in German: one of the advantages of living in your town/village, and one of disadvantages. Try to make them of equal length!

Foundation

Wo verbringst du normalerweise deine Ferien?
Where do you normally spend your holidays?
Ich verbringe meine Ferien normalerweise in Spanien/zu Hause.
I normally spend my holidays in Spain/at home.

Was hast du dort gemacht?
What did you do there?
Wir sind jeden Tag schwimmen gegangen, und am Abend sind wir in die Disco gegangen.
We went swimming every day and in the evening we went to the disco.

Wohin fährst du dieses Jahr in Urlaub? Wann? Für wie lange? Mit wem?
Where are you going for your holidays this year? When? For how long? With whom?
Im August fahre ich für zwei Wochen mit meiner Familie nach Wales.
In August I am going to Wales for 2 weeks with my family.

Wie war das Wetter?
What was the weather like?
Es war sonnig und warm.
It was sunny and warm.

Wo hast du gewohnt?
Where did you stay?
Wir haben in einem kleinen Hotel gewohnt.
We stayed in a small hotel.

Was hast du in den letzten Sommerferien gemacht?
What did you do in the last Summer holidays?
Ich bin mit Freunden nach Griechenland gefahren.
I went to Greece with friends.

Wie bist du gefahren?
How did you travel?
Wir sind geflogen. We flew.

Vocabulary

die Ferien / der Urlaub	-	holidays	kühl	- cool, fresh
die Sommerferien	-	summer holidays	bedeckt	- overcast
Zu Ostern	-	at Easter	nass	- wet
zur Weihnachtszeit	-	at Christmas	kalt	- cold
in den Herbstferien	-	during October half-term	neblig	- foggy
zu Hause	-	at home	regnerisch	- rainy
im Ausland	-	abroad	trocken	- dry
ins Ausland fahren	-	to go abroad	regnen	- to rain
der Zoll	-	customs	frieren	- to freeze
an der Küste	-	by the sea, on the coast	scheinen	- to shine
in den Alpen	-	in the Alps	die Sonne scheint	- the sun is shining
in den Bergen	-	in the mountains	schneien	- to snow
am Strand	-	on the beach	donnern und blitzen	- to thunder and lighten
sich sonnen / in der Sonne liegen	-	to sunbathe	das Gewitter / der Sturm	- storm
die Ansichtskarte	-	picture postcard	der Regen	- rain
das Wetter	-	the weather	der Schauer	- shower
es ist/war	-	it is/was	der Wind	- wind
warm	-	warm	der Schnee	- snow
sonnig	-	sunny	die Temperatur	- temperature
windig	-	windy	der Grad	- degree
wolkig	-	cloudy	der Wetterbericht	- weather report
herrlich	-	wonderful	die Wettervorhersage	- weather forecast

Higher

Erzähle mir von den letzten Sommerferien.
Tell me about your holidays last summer.
Letztes Jahr bin ich mit meiner Familie nach Frankreich gefahren. Wir haben gezeltet. Tagsüber habe ich in der Sonne gelegen, und wir haben auch viele Ausflüge gemacht. Wir haben sehr nette Leute kennengelernt und das Wetter war herrlich.
Last year I went with my family to France. We camped. During the day I sunbathed and we also went on lots of excursions. We met some very nice people and the weather was wonderful.

Wenn du die Wahl hättest, wo würdest du deine Ferien verbringen?
If you had a free choice, where would you spend your holidays?
Wenn ich die Wahl hätte, würde ich meine Ferien auf einer ruhigen Insel in der Karibik verbringen, weil ich gern in der Sonne liege, aber ich muss auch meine Ruhe haben.
If I had a free choice, I would spend my holidays on a peaceful island in the Caribbean, because I enjoy sunbathing, but I also need peace and quiet.

Grammar

The Perfect Tense with SEIN

We have already met examples of the perfect tense with HABEN as the auxiliary verb (see page 29). The topic of Holidays gives us the opportunity to look at verbs which have the auxiliary verb SEIN in the perfect tense. (to remind yourself of the verb SEIN, see page 9).

e.g. Ich bin nach Griechenland geflogen - I flew to Greece
Wir sind mit dem Auto gefahren - we went by car
Meine Freunde und ich sind in die Disco gegangen - my friends and I went to the disco

Verbs which take SEIN are usually verbs of MOVEMENT or TRAVEL, or a CHANGE OF STATE (e.g. das Wetter war am ersten Tag ganz warm, aber dann ist es kälter geworden - the weather was quite warm on the first day, but then it got colder).

Note this exception:
Ich bin zu Hause geblieben - I stayed at home

All examples of verbs with SEIN shown here have irregular past participles, which just have to be learnt! See the Verb Table pages 92-93 for more examples.

The Rule of Time, Manner, Place

Word order in German is governed by the rule of TIME, MANNER, PLACE as in the following examples:
Wir sind letztes Jahr (time) mit dem Auto (manner) nach Wales (place) gefahren.
Last year we went to Wales by car.
Nächsten April (time) fahre ich mit einer Schulgruppe (manner) nach Deutschland (place).
Next April I am going to Germany on a school trip.

This rule applies to all tenses.

Mini Test

Record yourself on tape talking about a holiday in the past, and plans for your next holiday.
Pay careful attention to tenses and include as much detail as possible.

Foundation

Gute Nacht, schlaf gut.
Goodnight, sleep well.

Tag Daniel. Willkommen in Deutschland!
Wie war die Reise?
Hello Daniel. Welcome to Germany!
How was the journey?
Danke, die Reise war ein bisschen anstrengend.
Thank you, the journey was a bit tiring.

Am Tisch.
At Table.
Guten Appetit.
Enjoy your meal.
Isst du gern Bohnen?
Do you like beans?
Ja ich esse sie gern.
Yes I like them.
Möchtest du noch etwas essen?
Would you like some more to eat?
Ja, bitte. Es schmeckt sehr gut.
Yes please. It tastes delicious.
Also, bedien dich.
Help yourself then.
Kannst du mir bitte das Brot geben?
Can you pass me the bread please?

Hast du Hunger/Durst?
Are you hungry/thirsty?
Nein danke, aber ich bin sehr müde.
No thank you, but I am very tired.
Also, ich zeige dir dein Zimmer.
I'll show you your bedroom then.

Wo ist das Badezimmer bitte?
Where is the bathroom please?
Direkt gegenüber deinem Zimmer.
Das grüne Handtuch ist für dich.
Directly opposite your room.
The green hand towel is for you.

Ich habe meinen Föhn vergessen.
I've forgotten my hair dryer.
Kein Problem. Du kannst meinen Föhn ausleihen.
No problem. You can borrow mine.

Vocabulary

der Austausch	-	exchange visit	die Mahlzeit	- meal
der Brieffreund/die-in	-	penfriend (m/f)	zeigen	- to show
willkommen	-	welcome	das Handtuch	- handtowel
(sich) vorstellen	-	to introduce (oneself)	das Badetuch	- bath towel
kennen/lernen	-	to meet, get to know	ausleihen	- to lend, borrow
die Reise	-	journey	das Shampoo	- shampoo
die Überfahrt	-	crossing	der Wecker	- alarm clock
stürmisch	-	stormy	die Seife	- soap
aus/packen	-	to unpack	die Zahnpasta	- tooth paste
zu Hause an/rufen	-	to call, telephone home	die Zahnbürste	- tooth brush
Hunger haben / hungrig sein	-	to be hungry	der Föhn	- hair dryer
			sich bedienen	- to help, serve oneself
Durst haben / durstig sein	-	to be thirsty	ich weiß nicht	- I don't know
			ich verstehe nicht	- I don't understand
müde	-	tired	es tut mir Leid	- I'm sorry
anstrengend	-	tiring	Entschuldigung	- excuse me, sorry
satt	-	full up (after meal)	wie bitte?	- pardon?
das Frühstück	-	breakfast	wie sagt man...	how do you say...
das Mittagessen	-	lunch	...auf Deutsch?	- ...in German?
das Abendessen / das Abendbrot	-	evening meal	...auf Englisch?	...in English?

Higher

Vielen Dank für Ihre Gastfreundschaft Frau Schmidt. Hoffentlich darf ich irgendwann wiederkommen.
Thank you very much for your hospitality Frau Schmidt. I hope I may come again some day.
Natürlich. Du bist immer willkommen bei uns.
Of course. You are always welcome here.

Mutti, darf ich dir meinen englischen Brieffreund James vorstellen?
Mum, may I introduce my English penfriend James?
Herzlich willkommen in Deutschland James.
Welcome to Germany James.
Danke. Es freut mich, Sie kennen zu lernen. Darf ich zu Hause anrufen?
Thank you. I'm pleased to meet you. May I phone home?

Wie war die Überfahrt James?
How was the crossing James?
Die Überfahrt war stürmisch. Viele Leute waren seekrank.
The crossing was stormy. Lots of people were seasick.

Was willst du heute nachmittag machen?
Willst du zu Hause bleiben, oder willst du ausgehen?
What do you want to do this afternoon?
Do you want to stay at home, or go out?
Ich möchte das Fußballspiel im Fernsehen angucken.
I'd like to watch the football match on TV.

Wann müssen wir morgen früh aufstehen?
What time do we have to get up tomorrow morning?
Morgen ist Schule, also müssen wir um Viertel vor sieben aufstehen.
We've got school tomorrow, so we have to get up at quarter to 7.

Guten Morgen James. Hast du gut geschlafen?
Good morning James. Did you sleep well?
Danke ja. Ich habe sehr gut geschlafen.
Yes thank you. I slept very well.

Grammar

Modal Verbs (2)

We met modal verbs on page 31. Here are some further examples of their use:
dürfen (to be allowed to), müssen (to have to) and wollen (to want to)

e.g. Darf ich zu Hause anrufen? Ja, du darfst!
May I ring home? Yes, you may!
Was willst du heute abend machen? Ich will zuerst auspacken.
What do you want to do this evening? I want to unpack first.
Wann muss ich morgen aufstehen? Du musst ziemlich früh aufstehen.
What time do I have to get up tomorrow? You have to get up quite early.

 Remember: that the modal verb is used together with another verb which is at the end of the clause/sentence in the INFINITIVE.

Mini Test

1. Think of 5 polite phrases you might use in German when staying with a family.
2. Practise making requests in German.

Foundation

Wann ist das Museum auf?
When is the museum open?
Jeden Tag außer Montag von 9 bis 5.
Every day except Monday from 9 till 5.
Wie komme ich dorthin?
How do I get there?
Ich zeige es Ihnen auf dem Stadtplan ...
I'll show you on the map ...

Haben Sie einen Stadtplan?
Do you have a plan of the town?
Ja, bitte schön.
Yes, here you are.

Ich möchte auch eine Liste von Hotels.
I would also like a list of hotels.
Bitte sehr. Here you are.

Ich suche einen Busfahrplan.
I'm looking for a bus timetable.
Die Fahrpläne sind dort drüben.
The timetables are over there.

Gibt es Ausflüge mit dem Bus?
Are there any coach trips?
Es gibt jeden Tag Ausflüge mit dem Bus.
There are coach trips every day.
Der Bus fährt von dem Marktplatz ab.
The coach departs from the
market place.

Können Sie mir Informationen
über Museen geben?
Can you give me some information
about museums?
Diese Broschüre hat Informationen
über die Sehenswürdigkeiten.
This brochure contains information
about the tourist attractions.

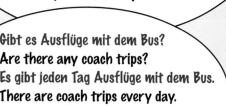

Was kostet das? How much is that?
Das ist umsonst. It's free.

Vocabulary

das Verkehrsamt das Informationsbüro	Tourist Information Office	das Schloss	castle
		die Burg	castle
der Stadtplan	map of the town	das Gebäude	building
die Broschüre	brochure	die Kunstgalerie	art gallery
der Prospekt	leaflet	die Fußgängerzone	pedestrian area
kostenlos umsonst gratis	free	der Ausflug	trip, excursion
		die Bootsfahrt	boat trip
		die Sehenswürdigkeiten	tourist attractions
die Liste	list	das Museum	museum
von Hotels von Gasthöfen von Gasthäusern	of hotels	der Turm	tower
		das Rathaus	town hall
		der Zoo	zoo
von Pensionen	of guest houses	das Denkmal	monument
von Campingplätzen	of campsites	besichtigen	to tour, have a look round, visit
von Restaurants	of restaurants	mieten	to hire
die Unterkunft	accommodation	außer	except
der Busfahrplan	bus timetable	die Ermäßigung	reduction
der Zugfahrplan	train timetable	die Gruppenermäßigung	group reduction
die Stadttour	tour of the town	einen Besuch wert	worth a visit
die Kathedrale	cathedral	empfehlen	to recommend
der Dom	cathedral		

Higher

Wäre es möglich, hier Fahrräder zu mieten?
Would it be possible to hire bikes here?
Nein, aber man kann sie vom Fahrradverleih neben dem Bahnhof mieten.
No, but you can hire them next to the railway station.

Ich würde gern wissen, was es hier für Unterkunftsmöglichkeiten gibt.
I would like to know what accommodation is available here.
Dieses Heftchen enthält viele Informationen.
This little booklet contains lots of information.

Ich möchte wissen, ob es eine Ermäßigung für Studenten gibt.
I would like to know if there is a reduction for students.
Ja, haben Sie Ihren Ausweis mit?
Yes, do you have your I.D. card with you?

Könnten Sie mir ein gutes Hotel empfehlen?
Could you recommend a good hotel?
Das Hotel Adler liegt in der Stadtmitte und ist nicht zu teuer.
The Adler Hotel is in the town centre, and is not too expensive.

Hätten Sie vielleicht einige Prospekte auf Englisch?
Would you have any leaflets in English by any chance?
Es tut mir Leid, wir haben keine übrig.
I'm sorry, we have none left.

Note that the content here is very similar to Foundation level but phrased in a more polite way by using the conditional tense (see grammar section below)

Grammar

The Conditional

The conditional tense is used to express what you **WOULD** do **IF** ..., or when making a polite request: **WOULD/COULD** you...?

The conditional tense in German is formed by using würde (with appropriate verb ending) and an infinitive at the end of the clause/sentence:

e.g. Welches Hotel würden Sie empfehlen? - **Which hotel would you recommend?**
Ich würde sehr dankbar sein. - **I would be very grateful.**

HABEN, SEIN and the **MODAL** verbs tend to use the imperfect subjunctive to express the conditional, rather than würde + an infinitive. For GCSE purposes, you do not have to worry about the formation of the imperfect subjunctive, simply be able to recognise and use the following:

e.g. Wenn ich mehr Zeit HÄTTE, würde ich die Altstadt besichtigen. - **If I had more time, I would visit the old part of town.**

Wenn ich morgen hier WÄRE, würde ich einen Ausflug machen. - **If I were here tomorrow, I would go on a trip.**

KÖNNTEN Sie mir sagen, wann die Geschäfte aufhaben? - **Could you tell me when the shops are open?**
Wir SOLLTEN eigentlich das Rathaus besichtigen; das soll einen Besuch wert sein.
We ought really to have a look around the town hall: it is supposed to be worth a visit.

Mini Test

1. Practise asking for different things at the Tourist Information Office, using the examples given on these two pages, and vary the way in which you ask for things.

Foundation

Wo ist die Post bitte?
Where is the post office please?
Gehen Sie ungefähr zweihundert Meter weiter,
und die Post ist auf der linken Seite.
**Carry on for about 200 metres, and the
post office is on the left hand side.**

Entschuldigen Sie, ich bin hier
fremd. Ich suche die Polizeiwache.
**Excuse me, I don't know my way
around here. I'm looking for
the police station.**
Gehen Sie hier die Straße entlang
bis zur Ampel. Dann gehen Sie links,
und die Polizeiwache ist auf der
rechten Seite.
**Go along the street here to the
traffic lights. Then turn left
and the police station is on
the right hand side.**

Wie komme ich am besten zum
Bahnhof/zur Jugendherberge bitte?
**How do I get to the railway station/youth
hostel please?**
Nehmen Sie die erste Straße links und dann
die zweite Straße rechts.
**Take the first street on the left and
then the second street on the right.**

Gibt es eine Bank in der Nähe?
Is there a bank nearby?
Ja, es gibt eine Bank gleich hier an der Ecke.
Yes, there is a bank just here on the corner.

Ist das Rathaus weit von hier?
Is the town hall far from here?
Nein, es ist zwei Minuten zu Fuß
entfernt. Gehen Sie hier geradeaus, und
es ist gegenüber dem Marktplatz.
**No, it's 2 minutes by foot. Carry straight
on, and it is opposite the market square.**

BANK

Vocabulary

Gehen Sie links...	-	go left		auf der linken Seite	-	on the left hand side
...rechts	-	right		auf der rechten Seite	-	on the right hand side
...geradeaus	-	straight on				
				Gehen Sie...		
Nehmen Sie die...				...die Straße hinauf	-	go up the street
...erste	-	take the first		...die Straße hinunter	-	down the street
...zweite	-	second		...die Straße entlang	-	along the street
...dritte Straße	-	third street				
				an der Ampel	-	at the lights
Gehen Sie...				an der Kreuzung	-	at the crossroads
...bis zur Ampel	-	carry on to the traffic lights		an der Ecke	-	on the corner
...bis zur Kreuzung	-	to the crossroads		die Polizeiwache	-	police station
...bis zur Brücke	-	to the bridge		die Stadtmitte ⎫		
...bis zum Marktplatz	-	to the market square		das Stadtzentrum ⎭	-	town centre
				das Schild	-	sign, signpost
Gehen Sie...				ab/biegen	-	(in car) to turn
...über die Brücke	-	cross the bridge				(off, into another road)
...über die Kreuzung	-	over the crossroads		zu Fuß	-	by foot
				...in Richtung	-	in the direction of

Higher

Wie komme ich am besten zum Bahnhof bitte, mit dem Bus oder zu Fuß?
What is the best way of getting to the railway station please, by bus or on foot?
Es ist schneller und einfacher, wenn Sie mit dem Bus fahren.
It is quicker and easier to go by bus.

Entschuldigen Sie bitte. Wie fahre ich am besten in die Stadtmitte?
Excuse me please. What is the best way of driving into town?
Biegen Sie hier links ab, und dann folgen Sie den Schildern bis zur Stadtmitte.
Turn left here, and then follow the signposts to the town centre.

Ich habe das nicht verstanden. Könnten Sie das bitte wiederholen?
I didn't understand that. Could you please repeat it?
Ja, gerne. Biegen Sie hier...
Yes of course. Turn...

Grammar

The Imperative (Commands)

There are four forms of command in German. Three are connected with the different forms of "you" - du, ihr, and Sie. The fourth is the first person plural "let's ..."

weak verb - spielen

du spielst	- you play	spiele!	- play! (remove "du", the "st" from the verb and add "e")
ihr spielt	- you play	spielt!	- play! (remove "ihr")
Sie spielen	- you play	spielen Sie!	- play! (invert subject and verb)
wir spielen	- we play	spielen wir!	- let's play! (invert subject and verb)

strong verb - gehen

du gehst	- you go	geh! *	- go!
ihr geht	- you go	geht!	- go!
Sie gehen	- you go	gehen Sie!	- go!
wir gehen	- we go	gehen wir!	- Let's go!

ZUM AND ZUR
Remember: that zu dem can be shortened to zum and zu der to zur.

* The "e" of the "du" command is frequently dropped in conversation, and with the following verbs:
- kommen, gehen, stehen, and lassen. It is also dropped in strong verbs when there is a vowel change to "i" or "ie" in the present tense : geben - gib!   lesen - lies!

Mini Test

Imagine you are directing a German tourist around your town. Direct him/her from a particular point to 5 places he/she may need to go, e.g. bank, post office.

Foundation

Wie fahre ich am besten zum Zoo?
What is the best way of getting to the zoo?
Sie fahren am besten mit der U-Bahn Linie eins Richtung Ruhleben.
Sie steigen am Bahnhof Zoo aus.
The best way is by underground, line 1 in the direction of Ruhleben.
You get off at Bahnhof Zoo.

Wie oft fährt der Bus Linie achtundsechzig bitte?
How frequent is the number 68 bus please?
Jede halbe Stunde - der nächste fährt in fünf Minuten.
Every half-hour - the next one leaves in 5 minutes.
Wo ist die nächste Bushaltestelle?
Where is the nearest bus stop?
Gerade hier vor der Bank.
Just here, in front of the bank.

Was kostet das für zwei Erwachsene und zwei Kinder zweiter Klasse hin und zurück bitte?
What does that cost for 2 adults and 2 children second class return?
Das macht zusammen hundertzwanzig Euros bitte.
All together that comes to 120 Euros.

Wann fährt der nächste Zug nach Hamburg bitte?
What time does the next train for Hamburg depart?
Um zehn Uhr fünfundfünfzig.
At 10.55.
Und von welchem Gleis?
And from which platform?
Von Gleis sieben.
From platform 7.

Wann kommt der Zug in Hamburg an?
What time does the train arrive in Hamburg?
Um zwölf Uhr dreiundvierzig.
At 12.43.

Fährt der Zug direkt, oder muss ich umsteigen?
Does the train go straight through, or do I have to change?
Nein, der Zug fährt direkt.
No, it's a direct line.

Vocabulary

mit dem Bus	-	by bus
mit dem Auto	-	by car
mit dem Zug		
mit der Bahn	} -	by train
mit der U-Bahn	-	by underground
mit der Straßenbahn	-	by tram
mit der S-Bahn	-	by suburban railway
mit dem Flugzeug	-	by plane
mit dem Schiff	-	by boat
mit der Fähre	-	by ferry
mit dem Luftkissenboot	-	by hovercraft
mit dem Mofa	-	by moped
mit dem Motorrad	-	by motor bike
fahren	-	to go, travel
reisen	-	to travel
die Reise	-	journey
die Bushaltestelle	-	bus stop
die U-Bahnstation	-	underground railway station
ein/steigen	-	to get on
aus/steigen	-	to get off
um/steigen	-	to change
der Flug	-	flight
die Fahrkarte	-	ticket
der Fahrschein	-	ticket
der Fahrkartenschalter	-	ticket office
der Inter-City-Zug	-	intercity train
der Zuschlag	-	supplement (payable on IC trains)
die Ankunft	-	arrival
die Abfahrt	-	departure
erster Klasse	-	1st class
zweiter Klasse	-	2nd class
der Platz	-	seat
der Hafen	-	port
der Flughafen	-	airport
DB - Deutsche Bundesbahn	-	the German Railway system
die Verspätung	-	delay
Raucher	-	smoking
Nichtraucher	-	non-smoking
einfach	-	single
hin und zurück	-	return
die Rückfahrkarte	-	return ticket
die öffentlichen Verkehrsmittel	-	public transport
das Gepäck	-	luggage
die Gepäckausgabe	-	left-luggage office/luggage reclaim
die Mehrfahrtenkarte	-	multi-journey ticket

Higher

Erzähl mir von einer langen Reise, die du gemacht hast.
Tell me about a long journey you have made.
Letztes Jahr bin ich mit einer Schulgruppe nach Deutschland gefahren. Wir sind mit dem Bus nach Harwich gefahren und dann mit dem Schiff nach Hamburg. An Bord haben wir gegessen, Karten gespielt und geschlafen. Die Überfahrt hat einundzwanzig Stunden gedauert, und wir waren alle müde, als wir in Hamburg angekommen sind.
Last year I went on a school trip to Germany. We went by coach to Harwich and then by boat to Hamburg. On board we ate, played cards and slept. The crossing took 21 hours and we were all tired when we arrived in Hamburg.

Sollte man weniger Auto fahren?
Should we use our cars less?
Um die Luftverschmutzung zu reduzieren, sollten wir versuchen, das Auto weniger zu benutzen - besonders wenn man nur eine kurze Strecke fährt. Dann kann man zu Fuß gehen, oder die öffentlichen Verkehrsmittel benutzen.
In order to reduce air pollution, we should try to use the car less - especially for short journeys. One can walk, or use public transport.

Grammar

UM .... ZU   (In order to ....)

The expression "in order to do something" is formed in German by using **um + zu** and the infinitive:

e.g. um Luftverschmutzung zu reduzieren, sollte man weniger Auto fahren
     in order to reduce air pollution, one should use one's car less
     um die Stadt so billig wie möglich zu sehen, sollte man eine 24-Stundenkarte kaufen
     in order to see the town as cheaply as possible, you should buy a 24 hour travel ticket.

Note the position of "zu" with separable verbs:
     um rechtzeitig anzukommen, müssen wir mit dem Taxi fahren
     in order to get there on time, we'll have to go by taxi

Mini Test

1. Practise asking questions related to bus and train travel - how many different questions can you think of?
2. Describe the public transport system in your town. How often do buses and trains run and to how many destinations? How expensive is it to use public transport?

Foundation

Volltanken bitte mit bleifrei/Ich möchte dreißig Liter Super bitte.
Fill the tank please, with lead free/I would like 30 litres of 4 star petrol please.

Vorsicht!
Look out!
Entschuldigung. Sind Sie verletzt?
I'm sorry. Are you hurt?
Mein Bein tut weh.
My leg hurts.
Ich werde die Polizei und einen Krankenwagen anrufen.
I'm going to ring for the police and an ambulance.

Verkaufen Sie Landkarten?
Do you sell maps?
Ja, und auch Getränke, Zeitungen, Süßigkeiten ...
Yes, and also drinks, newspapers, sweets ...

Könnten Sie bitte die Reifen/das Öl/das Wasser prüfen?
Could you check the tyres/oil/water please?
Ich habe alles geprüft.
Sie brauchen Öl.
I've checked everything.
You need some oil.

Ich habe eine Panne. Ich bin auf der Autobahn eins Richtung Bremen zwei Kilometer von Oberneuland entfernt. Können Sie jemanden schicken?
I've broken down on the A1 (motorway) in the direction of Bremen, 2 km from Oberneuland. Can you send someone?
Was für ein Auto ist es?
What kind of a car is it?
Ein blauer VW Golf Kennzeichen B425 ZJX.
A blue VW golf, registration number B425 ZJX
Wir sind in 10 Minuten da.
We'll be there in 10 minutes.

Vocabulary

die Tankstelle	-	petrol station	Lkw-Lastkraftwagen	-	heavy goods vehicle
Benzin	-	petrol	der Scheinwerfer	-	headlight
Super	-	4 star	die Reparaturwerkstatt	-	garage
bleifrei	-	lead free	der Abschleppwagen	-	recovery vehicle
verbleit	-	leaded	die Bremsen	-	brakes
unverbleit	-	unleaded	der Unfall	-	accident
die Landkarte	-	map	verletzt	-	injured
prüfen	-	to check	die Polizei	-	police
das Öl	-	oil	das Krankenwagen	-	ambulance
die Reifen	-	tyres	die Feuerwehr	-	fire service
der Reifendruck	-	tyre pressure	der LKW-Fahrer	-	lorry driver
brauchen	-	to need	der Lastwagen	-	lorry
der Parkplatz	-	car park or parking space	zusammen/stoßen	}	
eine Panne haben	-	to break down	prallen	}	to collide
das Kennzeichen	-	registration number	bremsen	-	to brake
der Motor	-	engine	überholen	-	to overtake
ADAC	-	equivalent to AA or RAC	ins Schleudern geraten	-	to skid
die Autobahn	-	motorway	die Spur wechseln	-	to change lanes
die Raststätte	-	service area	beschädigt	-	damaged
Pkw-Personenkraftwagen	-	car	nass	-	wet

Higher

Es ist ein Unfall auf der Autobahn nach Heidelberg passiert.
There has been an accident on the motorway to Heidelberg.
Was ist passiert? What happened?
Ein Lastwagen wollte ein Auto überholen, aber es regnete und der LKW-Fahrer konnte nicht gut sehen. Er ist ins Schleudern geraten, und ist gegen das Auto geprallt. Er hat sich das Bein gebrochen.
A lorry wanted to overtake a car, but it was raining and the lorry driver couldn't see very well. He skidded, and collided with the car. He broke his leg.

Herr Ziemer musste um neun bei einem Termin sein, also fuhr er ein bisschen zu schnell. Er wollte die Spur wechseln, und stieß plötzlich mit einem Motorrad zusammen. Er konnte nicht bremsen - er hatte keine Zeit. Glücklicherweise war niemand verletzt, aber das Auto wurde beschädigt.
Mr. Ziemer had to be at an appointment for 9.00, and so he drove a little too quickly. He wanted to change lane, and then suddenly collided with a motor bike. He couldn't brake - he didn't have the time. Luckily no-one was injured, but his car was damaged.

Grammar

The Imperfect Tense

We have already met the perfect tense in German (see pages 29 and 33), which is used in conversation and letter-writing for talking/writing about recent events in the past. The IMPERFECT tense in German is mainly a narrative tense, used for telling a story or writing an account of something.

Some very common verbs are nearly always used in the imperfect INSTEAD of the perfect tense. These are: haben, sein, werden and the modal verbs.

e.g. Ich musste um neun da sein
I had to be there for 9 o'clock
Ich konnte nicht bremsen
I could not apply the brakes
Er wollte das Auto überholen
He wanted to overtake the car

Ich hatte keine Zeit zu bremsen
I had no time to brake
Die Straßen waren nass
The roads were wet

The imperfect tense of **WEAK** verbs is formed in the following way:
take the stem of the infinitive and add the following endings:

machen - to do, make   mach (stem)   imperfect - ich machte   wir machten
                                             du machtest   ihr machtet
                                             er/sie/es machte   Sie/sie machten

Strong Verbs

Take the imperfect stem of the verb (see Verb Table pages 92-93) and add the following endings:

fahren - to go, drive   imperfect stem - fuhr   ich fuhr   wir fuhren
                                                    du fuhrst   ihr fuhrt
                                                    er/sie/es fuhr   Sie/sie fuhren

There are no endings added to the stem of the ich or er/sie/es forms.

Mini Test

1. Imagine you have broken down in a car in Germany, on the motorway to Frankfurt, 10 km from Karlsruhe. Explain your location, describe your car and what is wrong with it in a telephone conversation to a mechanic.
2. Imagine you have witnessed a traffic accident. Explain in German what happened.

Foundation

Zwei Roggenbrote bitte.
2 loaves of rye bread please.
Es tut mir Leid, das Roggenbrot ist alle.
Wir haben Vollkornbrot.
I'm sorry, we have no rye bread left.
We have some wholemeal bread.
Ich nehme lieber sechs Brötchen bitte.
I would rather have 6 rolls please.

Kann ich Ihnen helfen? **Can I help you?**
Ich hätte gern ein halbes Kilo Tomaten,
ein Kilo Kartoffeln, und was kosten die Birnen bitte?
I would like half a kilo of tomatoes, a kilo of potatoes
and what do the pears cost please?
Sie kosten fünfunddreißig Cents das Stück.
They cost 35 Cents each.
Dann nehme ich bitte sechs Stück. Was kostet
das alles zusammen?
Then I'll take 6 please. What does
that cost altogether?

Was kann ich für Sie tun?
What can I do for you?
Ich möchte zwei Flaschen Mineralwasser
und eine Dose Frankfurter.
I would like 2 bottles of mineral water
and a tin of frankfurter sausages.
Bitte sehr. Ist das alles?
There you are. Is that all?
Haben Sie eine kleinere Dose? Ja? Dann
geben Sie mir bitte die kleine Dose.
Do you have a smaller tin? Yes? Then
give me the small tin please.

Verkaufen Sie Leberwurst?
Do you sell liver sausage?
Ja, wie viel möchten Sie?
Yes, how much would you like?
Zweihundert Gramm bitte. Es tut mir Leid,
ich habe kein Kleingeld.
200g. please. I'm sorry, I don't have any change.
Das ist in Ordnung. Sonst noch etwas?
That's OK. Anything else?
Nein danke. **No thank you.**

Vocabulary

das Geschäft / der Laden	- shop		Erdbeeren	- strawberries
der Markt	- market		Himbeeren	- raspberries
der Supermarkt	- supermarket		Kirschen	- cherries
die Bäckerei	- baker's		Birnen	- pears
die Fleischerei / die Metzgerei	- butcher's		Pfirsiche	- peaches
der Gemüsehändler	- greengrocer's		Trauben	- grapes
die Konditorei	- cake shop		Zitronen	- lemons
das Lebensmittelgeschäft	- grocer's		Obst	- fruit
Tomaten	- tomatoes		Gemüse	- vegetables
Kartoffeln	- potatoes		Wurst	- sausage
Karotten	- carrots		Leberwust	- liver sausage
Champignons / Pilze	- mushrooms		Schinken	- ham
Kohl	- cabbage		Salami	- salami
Blumenkohl	- cauliflower		Eier	- eggs
Zwiebeln	- onions		Käse	- cheese
Erbsen	- peas		Marmelade	- jam
Kopfsalat	- lettuce		das Brot	- bread
Bohnen	- beans		das Brötchen	- bread roll
Äpfel	- apples		der Kuchen	- cake
Apfelsinen / Orangen	- oranges		die Torte	- gateau
Bananen	- bananas		Kekse	- biscuits
			Chips	- crisps
			der Einkaufswagen	- shopping trolley
			das Pfand	- deposit (on bottle)

Higher

Kann ich Ihnen helfen? **Can I help you?**

Ja, ich brauche ein halbes Kilo Pfirsiche und zwei Stück Paprika.
Yes, I need half a kilo of peaches and 2 green peppers.

Aber diese Pfirsiche will ich nicht - die sind überreif.
But I don't want these peaches - they are overripe.

Welche möchten Sie also? **So which would you like?**

Ich nehme jene Pfirsiche - die sehen etwas besser aus.
I'll take those - they look better.

Ich habe diese Flasche Limonade heute
früh gekauft, aber sie läuft aus. Können Sie mir eine andere geben?
I bought this bottle of lemonade this morning but it is leaking. Can you replace it?

Kein Problem. Und vergessen Sie nicht, Sie bekommen ein Cent Pfand
für die Flasche zurück.
No problem. And don't forget, there is 1 Cent back on the bottle.

Grammar

Quantities

When discussing quantities in German, there is no translation of the word "of":

e.g. ein Kilo Birnen - **a kilo of pears**
eine Tüte Milch - **a carton of milk**
200 Gramm Räucherkäse - **200 g of smoked cheese**

die Flasche	- bottle		das Paket	- packet
die Dose	- tin		das Stück	- piece
das Glas	- jar		die Tafel	- bar (chocolate)
die Tube	- tube		ein halbes Kilo	- half a kilo
die Schachtel	- box		ein Liter	- litre

Demonstrative Adjectives

"This" and "that" are demonstrative adjectives. In German dieser can be used for "this" or "that".
Jener (that) is usually used in contrast to dieser:

e.g. Diese Melone ist überreif - ich nehme jene Melone
This melon is overripe - I'll take that melon.

In the plural diese and jene are translated by "these" and "those".

Dieser and jener are declined like der (see page 85)

Welcher

Welcher? (which?) is declined exactly like dieser, and is used in asking questions. It is an interrogative adjective.

e.g. Welche Tomaten möchten Sie?
Which tomatoes would you like?
Welches Paket möchten Sie, das große oder das kleine?
Which packet would you like, the big one or the small one?

Foundation

Haben Sie etwas Größeres?
Have you got a bigger size?
Leider nicht.
Unfortunately not.

Haben Sie die gleiche Bluse in Rot?
Have you got the same blouse in red?
Es tut mir Leid. Sie sind alle in Grau.
I'm sorry. They are all grey.

Möchten Sie die Bluse anprobieren?
Would you like to try the blouse on?
Nein danke. Die Farbe gefällt mir nicht.
No thank you. I don't like the colour.

Ich suche einen Pullover.
I'm looking for a pullover.
Welche Farbe?
What colour?
Ich suche etwas Blaues.
I'm looking for something blue.
Und welche Größe haben Sie?
What size are you?
Größe vierzig.
Size 40.

Darf ich diese Hose anprobieren?
May I try these trousers on?
Natürlich. Die Umkleidekabinen sind dort drüben.
Of course. The changing rooms are over there.
Ich nehme diese Hose. Sie passt mir gut.
I'll take these trousers. They fit nicely.

Vocabulary

der Anorak	anorak	gestreift	striped
die Bluse	blouse	kariert	checked
das Hemd	shirt	der Hut	hat
die Hose	pair of trousers	Handschuhe	gloves
die Jeans	pair of Jeans	die Kleider	clothes
die Shorts	pair of shorts	die Größe	size
der Pullover	pullover	die Farbe	colour
das T-Shirt	T shirt	blau	blue
die Jacke	jacket	rot	red
die Wolljacke	cardigan	grün	green
die Krawatte / der Schlips	tie	gelb	yellow
		schwarz	black
der Mantel	coat	weiß	white
das Kleid	dress	braun	brown
der Rock	skirt	grau	grey
Schuhe	shoes	rosa	pink
Socken	socks	lila	purple
Sandalen	sandals	dunkelbraun	dark brown
die Strumpfhose	tights	hellblau	light blue
der Anzug	suit	bunt	brightly coloured
der Badeanzug	swimsuit	aus Baumwolle	cotton
die Badehose	swimming trunks	aus Seide	(in) silk
der Schlafanzug	pyjamas	aus Wolle	in wool (woollen)
der Regenmantel	raincoat	aus Leder	(in) leather
orange (nfarbig)	orange	aus Plastik	(in) plastic

Higher

Werden Sie schon bedient?
Are you being served?
Ich suche ein lila Hemd. **I'm looking for a purple shirt.**
Wir haben diese hier aus Baumwolle, oder diese aus Seide.
We have these in cotton, or these in silk.
Dieses Hemd steht mir gut, aber es ist mir zu teuer.
Haben Sie etwas Billigeres?
This shirt suits me but it is too expensive.
Do you have anything cheaper?

Ich habe diesen Mantel gestern gekauft.
Es fehlt ein Knopf, und am Ärmel ist ein Fleck.
Darf ich ihn umtauschen?
**I bought this coat yesterday. There is a button
missing and a stain on the sleeve. Can I change it?**
Haben Sie die Quittung? Also, kein Problem.
Do you have the receipt? No problem then.

Grammar

Etwas/Nichts/Wenig/Viel + Adjective

Adjectives following these words take a capital letter and add "es" to the end.
e.g. Ich suche etwas Preiswertes
I'm looking for something reasonably priced

Comparative adjectives can be used in the same way:
e.g. Es tut mir Leid, wir haben nichts Billigeres.
I'm sorry, we don't have anything cheaper.

One exception to the capital letter rule is ander
e.g. Haben Sie nichts anderes?
Have you nothing else?

Colours

Remember that colours are adjectives and require an adjective ending when used in front of the noun, according to case and gender:

e.g. Ich suche einen blauen Pullover.
I am looking for a blue pullover.
Diese graue Hose steht mir gut.
These grey trousers really suit me.

The colours rosa and lila are invariable - that means they do not require an adjective ending, wherever they stand in the sentence.
e.g. Ich suche ein rosa T-Shirt und lila Socken.
I'm looking for a pink T shirt and purple socks.

And finally, colours used in the phrase "in red" ,"in yellow", in German require a capital letter:
e.g. Haben Sie dasselbe in Gelb?
Do you have the same in yellow?

Foundation

Ist die Konditorei noch offen?
Ich möchte Pralinen kaufen.
Is the cake shop still open? I would
like to buy some chocolates.
Ich glaube, sie ist jetzt geschlossen.
I think it is closed now.

Ich suche ein Geschenk für
meinen Bruder. Er ist dreizehn.
I'm looking for a present for my brother. He is 13.
Wir haben diese T-Shirts hier im Sonderangebot.
We have these T shirts here on special offer.

Wo finde ich bitte Sportartikel?
Where will I find sports equipment please?
Im Erdgeschoss.
On the ground floor.
Und Schmuck?
And jewellery?
Der Schmuck befindet sich im dritten Stock.
Jewellery is on the 3rd floor.

Ich brauche ein Geschenk für meine Eltern.
Was kann ich für sie kaufen?
I need a present for my parents.
What can I buy for them?
Wir haben viele preiswerte Geschenkartikel.
We have lots of good value items.
Gut. Dann schaue ich mich ein bisschen um.
Good. I'll have a look round then.
Sie müssen sich beeilen. Das Kaufhaus
macht in zehn Minuten zu.
You will have to hurry. The store closes
in 10 minutes.

Vocabulary

das Kaufhaus	-	department store	Pralinen	-	chocolates
die Abteilung	-	department	die Flasche	-	bottle
im Erdgeschoss	-	on the ground floor	Parfüm	-	perfume
im ersten/zweiten Stock	-	on the first/second floor	Wein	-	wine
im Untergeschoss	-	in the basement	die Kreditkarte	-	credit card
im Sonderangebot	-	special offer	der Rabatt	-	discount
der Sommerschlussverkauf	-	summer sale	preiswert	-	good value
die Auswahl	-	choice, selection	billig	-	cheap
der Schal	-	scarf	teuer	-	expensive
der Regenschirm	-	umbrella	die Sonnenbrille	-	sunglasses
das Poster	-	poster	die Armbanduhr	-	watch
der Becher	-	mug	der Schmuck	-	jewellery
die CD	-	CD	die Brieftasche	-	wallet
die Kassette	-	cassette	das Portemonnaie	-	purse
das Buch	-	book	der Teddybär	-	teddy bear
der Reiseführer	-	travel guide	die Puppe	-	doll
der Bleistift	-	pencil	das Geschenk	-	present
der Kuli	-	pen	das Souvenir	-	souvenir
der Topf	-	pot	die Rückzahlung	-	refund
die Schachtel	-	box	um/tauschen	-	to exchange (goods)

Higher

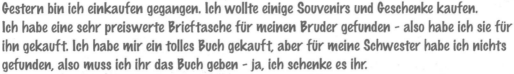

Ich habe diese Armbanduhr gestern gekauft
und sie geht nicht. Ich hätte gern mein Geld für diese Armbanduhr zurück.
I bought this wrist watch yesterday and it isn't working.
I would like a refund please.
Sie müssen zum Kundendienst gehen.
You will have to go to Customer Services.

Gestern bin ich einkaufen gegangen. Ich wollte einige Souvenirs und Geschenke kaufen.
Ich habe eine sehr preiswerte Brieftasche für meinen Bruder gefunden - also habe ich sie für
ihn gekauft. Ich habe mir ein tolles Buch gekauft, aber für meine Schwester habe ich nichts
gefunden, also muss ich ihr das Buch geben - ja, ich schenke es ihr.
Yesterday I went shopping for presents and souvenirs. I found a very reasonably-priced wallet for
my brother, so I bought it for him. I bought myself a great book, but I didn't find anything for
my sister so I will have to give her the book - yes, I shall give it to her as a present.

Grammar

Direct And Indirect Object Pronouns

Remember that a PRONOUN replaces a NOUN in a sentence:

Ich brauche ein Geschenk für <u>meine Eltern</u>.
Was kann ich für <u>sie</u> kaufen ?
I need a present for <u>my parents</u> (noun). What can I buy for <u>them</u>? (pronoun)
<u>Dieses Buch</u> sieht interessant aus. Ich werde <u>es</u> kaufen.
<u>This book</u> looks interesting. I shall buy <u>it</u>.

We looked at subject pronouns on page 9.
Here is the complete table with subject, direct object and indirect object pronouns:

<u>subject</u>	<u>direct object</u>	<u>indirect object</u>
ich - I	mich - me	mir - to me
du - you	dich - you	dir - to you
er - he, it	ihn - him, it	ihm - to him, it
sie - she, it	sie - her, it	ihr - to her, it
es - it	es - it	ihm - to it
wir - we	uns - us	uns - to us
ihr - you	euch - you	euch - to you
Sie - you	Sie - you	Ihnen - to you
sie - they	sie - them	ihnen - to them

Note word order when both DIRECT and INDIRECT OBJECT PRONOUNS ARE USED IN THE SAME SENTENCE:

Ich gebe meiner Mutter (indirect object) eine Flasche Parfüm (direct object) - I give my mother a bottle of perfume.
Ich gebe sie (direct object pronoun) meiner Mutter (indirect object) - I give it to my mother.
Ich gebe ihr (indirect object pronoun) eine Flasche Parfüm (direct object) - I give a bottle of perfume to her.
Ich gebe sie (direct object pronoun) ihr (indirect object pronoun) - I give it to her.

Mini Test

Write out a shopping list in German of presents and souvenirs that you would want to buy for various members
of your family. Choose a different present for each person and keep to a sensible budget!

Foundation

Im Café - In the café
Meine Damen, was darf es sein?
Ladies, what can I get you?
Ich nehme eine Limo und für meine Freundin eine Cola bitte.
I'll have a lemonade and a cola for my friend.

Ist hier in der Nähe eine Wurstbude? Ich muss schnell etwas essen.
Is there a hot dog stall nearby? I have to grab a bite to eat.
Nein, aber es gibt ein FastFood Restaurant gleich um die Ecke.
No, there's a fast food restaurant just around the corner.

Möchten Sie etwas essen?
Would you like something to eat?
Ja, ich bin hungrig. Ich hätte gern ein Käsebrot, und du?
Yes, I'm hungry. I would like a cheese sandwich, what about you?

In der Eisdiele - in the ice-cream parlour
Welche Eissorten haben Sie?
What flavours do you have?
Wir haben Vanilleeis oder Schokoladeneis.
We have vanilla or chocolate ice cream.
Zwei Kugeln Vanilleeis bitte.
2 scoops of vanilla ice cream please.

Ich esse gern Pizza.
Was für Pizza haben Sie?
I like pizza. What kind of pizza do you have?
Wir haben Pizza mit Schinken oder mit Champignons.
We have pizza with ham or mushrooms.

In der Imbissstube - in the snack bar
Eine Bockwurst und eine große Portion Pommes bitte.
One sausage and a large portion of chips please.
Mit Senf? **With mustard?**
Nein, mit Ketchup bitte. **No, with tomato sauce please.**

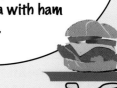

Vocabulary

das Café	-	café	Kakao	- cocoa
die Imbissstube	-	snack bar, café	Rotwein	- red wine
die Wurstbude	-	sausage/hot-dog stand	Weißwein	- white wine
die Eisdiele	-	ice-cream parlour	Erdbeereis	- strawberry ice cream
das Fast Food Restaurant	-	fast food restaurant	der Eisbecher	- ice cream sundae
der Imbiss	-	snack	Kaffee	- coffee
das Butterbrot	-	sandwich	Tee	- tea
das Käsebrot	-	cheese sandwich	mit Milch	- with milk
die Bockwurst	-	sausage (steamed)	mit Zitrone	- with lemon
die Bratwurst	-	sausage (fried)	Zucker	- sugar
die Currywurst	-	curry sausage	Sprudel	- fizzy mineral water
das Eis	-	ice cream	Limo, Limonade	- lemonade
die Kugel	-	scoop	Cola	- cola
die Portion	-	portion	Orangensaft	- orange juice
Sahne	-	cream	Apfelsaft	- apple juice
Vanilleeis	-	vanilla ice cream	Bier	- beer
Schokoladeneis	-	chocolate ice cream	vom Fass	- draught beer
das Gebäck	-	pastries, biscuits	eine Tasse	- a cup
die Schlagsahne	-	whipped cream	ein Kännchen	- a pot
			ein Glas	- a glass

Higher

Wo essen wir zu Mittag?
Where shall we have lunch?
Ich habe nicht viel Geld, also müssen wir eine Imbisstube finden, die nicht zu teuer ist.
I have not got a lot of money so we will have to find a cafeteria which is not too expensive.
Wie wäre es mit dem neuen Café, das du in der Hauptstraße gesehen hast?
What about the new café which you saw in the main street?
Gute Idee!
Good idea!

Wo ist der Kellner?
Where is the waiter?
Der Mann, der an der Theke steht, ist unser Kellner - Herr Ober!
The man standing at the counter is our waiter - Waiter!
Können Sie mir bitte eine andere Gabel bringen - diese ist schmutzig.
Can you bring me another fork please - this one is dirty.

Grammar

Relative Pronouns

Relative pronouns sometimes cause problems for English students of German, because in English we do not always use relative pronouns where in German they MUST be used.

e.g. Der Kellner, <u>der</u> an der Theke steht
The waiter standing by the counter (the waiter WHO is standing by the counter)
Die Kellnerin, <u>die</u> uns bedient hat
The waitress who served us
Das Mädchen, mit <u>dem</u> ich am Telefon gesprochen habe
The girl to whom I spoke on the phone

Note in the above examples that the relative pronoun will send the verb to the end of the relative clause, and that this relative clause is separated from the rest of the sentence by a comma.

The relative pronouns in English are: who, whom, which and that.
In German the relative pronouns are declined according to case and gender as follows:

	masculine	feminine	neuter	plural	
N	der	die	das	die	who, which
A	den	die	das	die	whom, which
G	dessen	deren	dessen	deren	whose, of which
D	dem	der	dem	denen	to whom/which

Mini Test

Order snacks, drinks and ice cream in German for a group of four people.

Foundation

Zahlen bitte!
We would like to pay please.
Zusammen oder getrennt?
Together or separately?
Getrennt bitte.
Separately please.

Haben Sie einen Tisch für vier Personen bitte?
Do you have a table for four please?
Ja, wir haben einen Tisch neben dem Fenster. Geht das?
Yes, we have a table next to the window. Is that OK?

Die Speisekarte bitte.
The menu please.
Bitte schön. Wir haben auch das Menü.
Here you are. We also have the fixed price menu.

Fräulein! Waitress!
Es fehlt ein Messer. There's a knife missing.
Und darf ich Salz und Pfeffer haben?
And may I have salt and pepper?

Herr Ober! Wir möchten bestellen.
Waiter! We are ready to order now.
Als Vorspeise möchte ich die Suppe.
As a starter I shall have the soup.

Und zu trinken?
And to drink?
Bringen Sie mir bitte die Weinliste.
Bring me the wine list please.
Kommt sofort.
I'll bring it immediately.

Und als Hauptgericht?
And for the main course?
Ich nehme Hähnchen und Bratkartoffeln.
I shall have chicken with fried potatoes
Und als Nachspeise nehme ich einen Eisbecher.
And for dessert I shall have an ice cream sundae.

Vocabulary

die Speisekarte	-	menu	der Knödel	-	dumpling
das Menü	-	fixed-price menu	Kartoffelsalat	-	potato salad
die Weinkarte / die Weinliste	-	wine list	das Sauerkraut	-	pickled cabbage
die Gulaschsuppe	-	goulash soup	der Fisch	-	fish
der Aufschnitt	-	cold meat	die Forelle	-	trout
das Spiegelei	-	fried egg	die Vorspeise	-	starter
das Omelett	-	omelette	das Hauptgericht	-	main course
das Fleisch	-	meat	die Nachspeise / der Nachtisch	-	dessert
das Hähnchen	-	chicken	die Gabel	-	fork
das Kotelett	-	chop	das Messer	-	knife
das Rindfleisch	-	beef	der Löffel	-	spoon
das Schweinefleisch	-	pork	der Pfeffer	-	pepper
der Eintopf	-	stew	das Salz	-	salt
Bratkartoffeln	-	fried potatoes	einschließlich/einschl.	-	inclusive
Salzkartoffeln	-	boiled potatoes	die Mehrwertsteuer	-	VAT

Higher

Zahlen bitte.
I'd like to pay please.
Hier ist die Rechnung.
Here is the bill.
Sind Bedienung und
Mehrwertsteuer inbegriffen?
Are service charge
and VAT included?

Guten Tag. Haben Sie einen Tisch frei?
Wir sind fünf Personen.
Hello. Do you have a table? There are 5 of us.
Ja. Wir haben diesen Tisch neben dem Fenster.
Yes. We have this table next to the window.
Wir möchten lieber draußen auf der Terrasse sitzen.
We would prefer to sit outside on the terrace.

Was empfehlen Sie heute?
What do you recommend today?
Das Eisbein ist sehr gut.
The "Eisbein" is very good.
Was ist das?
What is that?
Das ist Schweinefleisch, und wird mit
Sauerkraut serviert.
It is pork, and is served with sauerkraut.
Nein danke, ich esse kein Fleisch.
No thank you, I don't eat meat.

Hat es Ihnen geschmeckt?
Did you enjoy your meal?
Ja, danke. Es hat mir sehr
gut geschmeckt/Nein.
Die Suppe war kalt, das Fleisch war zu
fettig und die Soße war zu scharf.
Yes thank you. It was very tasty/No.
The soup was cold, the meat was too
fatty and the sauce was too spicy.

Grammar

Impersonal Verbs

Impersonal verbs always have "es" as the subject of the verb. Many impersonal verbs in German
take the dative:

e.g.   es gefällt mir - I like it
es tut mir Leid - I am sorry
es gelingt mir - I succeed
es tut mir weh - it hurts
es schmeckt (mir) - it tastes good

Gefällt es dir hier? - Do you like it here?
Hat es Ihnen geschmeckt? - Did you enjoy your meal?
Ihm tut die Hand weh - His hand hurts
Es ist ihr gelungen, Karten für das Bruce Springsteen Konzert zu bekommen.
She succeeded in getting tickets for the Bruce Springsteen concert.

Impersonal verbs are also used to describe the weather:
es regnet - it is raining
es schneit - it is snowing
es friert - it is freezing
es donnert und es blitzt - it is thundering and lightening

Mini Test

List as many items of food and drink as you can in the form of a menu in German. Using the menu you have made,
order yourself a 3 course meal.

Foundation

Wann gibt es Frühstück?
When is breakfast?
Zwischen acht und halb zehn.
Between 8.00 - 9.30.
Und wo ist der Speisesaal?
And where is the dining room?
Hier gegenüber dem Empfang.
Opposite reception.

Haben Sie noch Zimmer frei bitte?
Do you have any rooms available please?
Was für ein Zimmer möchten Sie?
What kind of room would you like?
Ich möchte ein Doppelzimmer mit Dusche und Balkon.
I would like a double room with a shower and balcony.

hotel

Für wie viele Nächte?
For how many nights?
Für eine Nacht/zwei Nächte.
For one night/two nights.

Gut. Dann nehme
ich das Zimmer.
Fine. I'll take the room.
Hier ist der Schlüssel.
Das ist Zimmernummer
elf im zweiten Stock.
**Here is the key. It is room
11 on the second floor.**
Gibt es einen Fahrstuhl?
Is there a lift?
Ja, hier links.
Yes, just on the left here.

Ist Frühstück im
Preis inbegriffen?
Is breakfast included?
Nein, Sie müssen extra
dafür bezahlen.
**No you have to pay
extra for it.**

Was kostet das Zimmer?
What does the room cost?
Das kostet dreißig Euros pro Person pro Nacht mit Frühstück.
That costs 30 Euros per person per night with breakfast.

Vocabulary

das Einzelzimmer	-	single room	das Laken	- sheet
das Doppelzimmer	-	double room	die Decke	- blanket
frei	-	free, available	der Wasserhahn	- tap
voll	-	full	die Zentralheizung	- central heating
mit Bad	-	with a bath	inbegriffen / inklusive	- included
mit Dusche	-	with a shower		
mit Balkon	-	with a balcony	Vollpension	- full board
mit Blick auf das Meer	-	with a sea view	Halbpension	- half board
mit Fernseher	-	with TV	Übernachtung	- overnight accommodation
mit Telefon	-	with a telephone	Frühstück	- breakfast
der Schlüssel	-	key	die Reservierung	- reservation
der Fahrstuhl / der Lift	-	lift	reservieren	- to reserve
			der Empfang	- reception
das Kopfkissen	-	pillow	sich beklagen / sich beschweren	- to complain
das Bettzeug	-	bedding		

Higher

Guten Tag. Ich habe ein Zimmer reserviert.
Hello. I have a room reserved.
Wie ist Ihr Name bitte?
What is the name please?
HILL ist der Name.
The name is HILL.
Und wann fahren Sie wieder ab?
And when are you leaving?
Übermorgen.
The day after tomorrow.

Ich möchte mich über mein Zimmer beklagen.
I would like to make a complaint about my room.
Was ist das Problem mein Herr?
What is the problem sir?
Es gibt mehrere! Gestern abend bin ich gerade eingeschlafen, als der Lärm von der Hotelbar mich geweckt hat, und ich konnte nicht wieder einschlafen. Dann ist heute früh kein warmes Wasser aus dem Wasserhahn gekommen. Ich hatte gerade mit dem Empfang wegen des Problems telefoniert, als der Fernseher kaputtgegangen ist.
There are several! Last night I had just gone to sleep when the noise from the hotel bar woke me up and I couldn't get to sleep again. Then this morning I had no hot water. I had just rung reception about the problem when the TV broke down.

Grammar

The Pluperfect Tense

 Remember: that the Perfect tense is used when talking about something that has happened in the past. The PLUPERFECT tense goes further back in time and expresses something that HAD happened prior to an action already in the past:

Ich hatte schon das Hotel verlassen, als mein Gepäck endlich angekommen ist.
I had already left the hotel, when my luggage finally arrived.
Der Manager war schon nach Hause gegangen, als ich ein drittes Problem mit meinem Zimmer entdeckt habe!
The manager had already gone home when I discovered a third problem with my room!

The pluperfect is formed in a similar way to the perfect tense, with a past participle and a part of HABEN or SEIN, but in the PLUPERFECT it is the IMPERFECT tense of HABEN or SEIN which is used: (See p.92 and p.93)

Ich habe das Hotel verlassen - I (have) left the hotel   **PERFECT TENSE**
Ich hatte das Hotel verlassen - I had left the hotel   **PLUPERFECT TENSE**

Mini Test

1. Book yourself into a luxury hotel with at least five facilities.
2. Imagine yourself in the worst hotel room ever and report all its faults to reception.

Foundation

Welche Mahlzeiten wollen Sie?
Which meals would you like?
Wir möchten Abendessen und Frühstück.
We would like evening meal and breakfast.
Gut. Der Jungenschlafraum ist hier links und der Mädchenschlafraum ist im ersten Stock.
Fine. The boys' dormitory is just here on the left, and the girls' dormitory is on the first floor.

Auf dem Campingplatz - **at the campsite**
Haben Sie Platz frei für ein Zelt und einen Wohnwagen bitte?
Do you have room for a tent and a caravan please?
Ja, wie lange wollen Sie bleiben?
Yes, for how long?
Drei Nächte. **3 nights.**

Wie viele Personen sind Sie?
How many people are there?
Wir sind zwei Erwachsene und zwei Kinder.
There are 2 adults and 2 children.

Können Sie bitte dieses Formular ausfüllen und hier unterschreiben?
Can you fill in this form and sign here?
Brauchen Sie Bettwäsche?
Do you need sheets and blankets?
Nein, wir haben Schlafsäcke mit.
No, we have our sleeping bags.

Bitte schön, das ist Platznummer neun gegenüber den Duschen.
Here you are, it is pitch number 9 opposite the showers.
Kann man hier kochen?
Can we do our own cooking here?
Ja, Campinggas erhalten Sie im Geschäft nebenan.
Yes, you can get camping gas from the shop next door.

In der Jugendherberge - **in the Youth Hostel**
Guten Abend. Wir brauchen drei Betten für heute abend.
Good evening. We need 3 beds for tonight.
Sie haben Glück. Wir haben noch Plätze frei.
Haben Sie Ihre Herbergsausweise mit?
You're lucky. We still have places available. Do you have your Youth Hostel membership cards with you?

Vocabulary

der Campingplatz	-	campsite	DJH		German Youth Hostel
das Zelt	-	tent	Deutsche Jugendherbergen	-	Association
der Wohnwagen	-	caravan	der Schlafraum	-	dormitory
der Platz	-	pitch, space	der Schlafsack	-	sleeping bag
die Duschen	-	showers	Bettwäsche	-	bedlinen
die Toiletten	-	toilets	der Aufenthaltsraum	-	recreation room
der Waschraum	-	washroom	der Ausweis	-	ID card
die Anmeldung	-	reception	das Mitglied	-	member
der Campinggas	-	camping gas	der Herbergsvater	-	male warden
der Campingkocher	-	camping stove	die Herbergsmutter	-	female warden
der Spielplatz	-	play area	das Formular	-	form
im Schatten	-	in the shade	ausfüllen	-	to fill in
zelten	-	to camp	unterschreiben	-	to sign
Strom	-	electricity	ausleihen	-	to hire
die Jugendherberge	-	youth hostel	verboten	-	forbidden
			erlaubt	-	permitted

Higher

Ich erkläre Ihnen schnell die Hausordnung:
Let me quickly explain the rules of the Youth Hostel to you:
Dir Türen werden um Mitternacht abgeschlossen. Nach zweiundzwanzig
Uhr muss man leise sprechen. Es ist streng verboten, Alkohol in
der Jugendherberge zu trinken.
The doors are closed at midnight. After 10pm you have to be quiet.
It is strictly forbidden to drink alcohol in the youth hostel.

Ich komme regelmäßig zu diesem Campingplatz, aber
dieses Jahr bin ich mit meinem Aufenthalt höchst unzufrieden.
I come to this campsite regularly, but this year I am extremely dissatisfied
with my stay.
Was ist das Problem, mein Herr?
What is the problem Sir?
Zuerst fiel der Strom aus. Dann mitten in der Nacht gab es viel Lärm,
und schließlich wurden die Waschräume selten saubergemacht.
First of all the electricity was faulty. Then in the middle of the night there
was a lot of noise and finally the washrooms were rarely cleaned.

Grammar

Adverbs

Adverbs are words which usually describe **VERBS**. They describe **WHEN, WHERE,** or **HOW** things happen. In English adverbs often end in '-ly'

Jedes Jahr komme ich nach Deutschland - **I come to Germany every year (when)**
Oben ist alles ruhig - **everything is quiet upstairs (where)**
Das hat er schnell gemacht - **he did that quickly (how)**

Adverbs may also be used with an adjective or another adverb
e.g. ein sorgfältig ausgefülltes Formular - **a carefully filled-in form**
er ist sehr langsam gefahren - **he drove very slowly**

Many adjectives can be used as adverbs in German. When used as adverbs, **THEY ARE INVARIABLE** i.e. **THEY DO NOT HAVE ANY CASE ENDINGS.** This in fact makes them much easier to use than adjectives, although they are often overlooked by GCSE candidates.

Note in the above example - "ein sorgfältig ausgefülltes Formular" that the adjective sorgfältig (careful) is being used as an adverb (carefully) and therefore does not have an ending, whilst the adjective ausgefülltes does. (ausgefüllt - past participle used as an adjective)

See Grammar Summary pages 86-87 for more on adverbs, including the comparative and superlative.

Mini Test

1. Practise arriving at a campsite/youth hostel and enquiring about availability of accommodation for different groups of people, with different requirements.
2. Put together 10 sentences in German, on any topic, including at LEAST one ADVERB in each sentence.

Foundation

Wo ist der Briefkasten bitte?
Where is the letter box please?
Gleich vorne - gegenüber dem Schalter.
**Just here in front of you,
opposite the counter.**

In der Bank - At the Bank
Guten Tag. Ich möchte bitte einen
Reisescheck zu fünfzig Pfund einlösen.
**Good morning. I would like to cash a
traveller's cheque for £50 please.**
Haben Sie Ihren Pass mit?
Do you have your passport?

Ich möchte diese Postkarten und dieses
Paket ins Ausland nach England schicken.
**I would like to send these postcards and
this parcel abroad to England please.**
Ich muss das Paket wiegen. Das kostet
sechs Euros dreißig insgesamt.
**I'll have to weigh the parcel. That comes
to 6 Euros 30 Cents altogether.**

Bitte schön. Wie ist der Kurs heute?
Here you are. What is the rate of exchange today?
Der Kurs ist heute ein Euro dreiundfünfzig Cents.
It is 1 Euro 53 Cents to the pound today.

Muss ich eine Gebühr bezahlen?
Do I have to pay a commission fee?
Ja, zwei Prozent. Können Sie bitte
hier unterschreiben?
Yes, it's 2%. Can you sign here please?

An der Post - At the Post Office
Was kostet ein Brief in die Schweiz?
What does a letter to Switzerland cost?
fünfundfünfzig Cents.
fifty five Cents.
Dann geben Sie mir bitte
drei Briefmarken zu
fünfundfünfzig Cents.
**Then give me 3 fifty five
Cents stamps please.**

Ja. Ich möchte auch
englisches Geld in Euros wechseln.
**Yes. I would also like to change some
English money into Euros.**
Wie viel möchten Sie wechseln?
How much would you like to change?

Vocabulary

Die Bank	-	bank
die Post } das Postamt }	-	post office
die Wechselstube	-	{ exchange bureau, bureau de change
der Reisescheck	-	traveller's cheque
das Geld	-	money
der Pass	-	passport
der Kurs	-	rate of exchange
die Banknote } der Bankschein }	-	banknote
die D-Mark	-	German mark
der Pfennig	-	pfennig
der Franken	-	Swiss franc
Der Euro	-	Euro
der Schilling	-	Austrian shilling
schicken	-	to send
wiegen	-	to weigh
das Paket	-	parcel
der Brief	-	letter

die Postkarte	-	postcard
die Briefmarke	-	stamp
der Briefmarkenautomat	-	stamp machine
der Briefkasten	-	letter box
ins Ausland schicken	-	to send abroad
Holland } Die Niederlande }	-	Holland
Belgien	-	Belgium
Amerika	-	America
Dänemark	-	Denmark
Frankreich	-	France
Griechenland	-	Greece
Großbritannien	-	Great Britain
Italien	-	Italy
Österreich	-	Austria
die Schweiz	-	Switzerland
Spanien	-	Spain
Köln	-	Cologne
München	-	Munich
Bayern	-	Bavaria
Wien	-	Vienna
Europa	-	Europe

BANK

Higher

Wäre es möglich, mit meiner Kreditkarte Geld einzulösen?
Would it be possible to withdraw money using my credit card?
Ja, wie möchten Sie das Geld?
Yes, how would you like the money?
Ich möchte zwei Fünfzigeuroscheine bitte.
I would like 2 x 50 Euro notes please.

Wie lange braucht die Post nach Österreich?
How long does it take for post to arrive in Austria?
Normalerweise dauert das drei Tage, aber seit letzter
Woche streiken dort die Postleute. Ich kann es Ihnen also nicht sagen.
**Normally it takes 3 days, but the postal workers over
there have been on strike since last week, so I can't really say.**

Grammar

Prepositions Governing The Dative

The following prepositions are always followed by the DATIVE case:

aus	-	out of, from
außer	-	except
bei	-	at the house of, near, with
gegenüber	-	opposite (often follows noun)
mit	-	with
nach	-	after, to (town, country, home), according to
seit	-	since, for (length of time)
von	-	from, of
zu	-	to, at

e.g. Er kommt aus der Schweiz - **he comes from Switzerland**
Bei mir - **at home, at my house, also - with me**
Der Post gegenüber - **opposite the post office**
Mit meiner Kreditkarte - **with my credit card**
Wir sind von Deutschland nach Österreich gefahren - **we travelled from Germany to Austria.**
Er ging zum Briefkasten - **he went to the post box**
Zu Weihnachten - **at Christmas**
Briefmarken zu 80 Pfennig - **80 pfennig stamps**

Note these shortened forms:

zu dem	-	zum
zu der	-	zur
bei dem	-	beim
von dem	-	vom

Mini Test

1. Practise conversations at the bank/exchange bureau dealing with cash transactions.
   Vary the currency - use Swiss francs or Austrian shillings.
2. You need to send postcards, letters and parcels to four different countries. Imagine the conversation at the post office.

Foundation

Kann man hier Fahrräder ausleihen?
Can we hire bikes here?
Ja, das kostet fünfzehn Euros pro Fahrrad ohne Kaution.
Yes, it costs 15 Euros per bike without the deposit.

Gibt es hier in der Nähe eine Reinigung.
Ich muss meine Jacke chemisch reinigen lassen.
Is there a dry-cleaner's nearby? I have to have my jacket dry-cleaned.
Ja, gehen Sie hier die Straße entlang, und die Reinigung ist gleich um die Ecke.
Yes, go along the street and the dry-cleaner's is just around the corner.

Im Friseursalon - At the Hairdresser's
Ich möchte mir die Haare schneiden lassen. Brauche ich einen Termin?
I would like my hair cut. Do I need an appointment?
Nein, das können wir gleich machen.
No, we can do that straight away.

Im Fundbüro - At the Lost Property Office
Können Sie mir helfen? Ich habe gestern meine Armbanduhr verloren.
Can you help me? I lost my watch yesterday.
Können Sie die Armbanduhr beschreiben?
Can you describe the watch?
Sie ist aus Silber und nagelneu.
It is silver and brand new.

Im Fotoladen - In the Photographer's
Kann ich hier meinen Photoapparat reparieren lassen?
Can I get my camera repaired here?
Lassen Sie mich mal sehen...Ja, kein Problem.
Let me see...yes, no problem.
Wie lange dauert das?
How long will it take?
Bis morgen.
It will be ready tomorrow.

Vocabulary

das Fahrrad/das Rad	-	bicycle	finden	-	to find
aus/leihen	-	to hire	vergessen	-	to forget
die Kaution	-	deposit	liegen/lassen	-	to leave behind
ein Auto mieten	-	to hire a car	fallen/lassen	-	to drop
die Versicherung	-	insurance	fertig	-	ready, finished
die Reinigung	-	dry-cleaner's	bis morgen	-	until tomorrow
der Fotoladen	-	photographer's	der Photoapparat	-	camera
das Fundbüro	-	lost property office	die Brille	-	pair of glasses
chemisch reinigen	-	to dry-clean	die Armbanduhr	-	wristwatch
reparieren	-	to repair	der Walkman	-	walkman
entwickeln	-	to develop	der Ring	-	ring
lassen + infinitive	-	to get something done	die Halskette	-	necklace
zerbrechen	-	to break	die Handtasche	-	handbag
zerbrochen kaputt	- broken		beschreiben	-	to describe
			aus Gold	-	gold
			aus Silber	-	silver
verlieren	-	to lose	aus Metall	-	metal

Higher

Ich möchte ein Auto für die ganze Woche ein Auto mieten.
I would like to hire a car for the entire week.
Können Sie bitte dieses Formular ausfüllen, und ich brauche
Ihren Führerschein und Ausweis. Der Preis hier ist ohne Versicherung.
**Can you please fill in this form and I also need your driving
licence and ID card. The price here does not include insurance.**

Ich habe meine Handtasche im
Bus liegenlassen. Können Sie mir helfen?
**I have left my handbag on the bus.
Can you help me?**
Wie sieht die Tasche aus?
What does the bag look like?
Sie ist ziemlich groß, dunkelbraun und
aus Leder. Darin sind meine Schlüssel,
mein Portemonnaie und mein Pass!
**It is quite big, dark brown and made of
leather. Inside are my keys, my purse
and my passport!**

Ich möchte meine Brille reparieren
lassen. Ich habe sie gestern fallenlassen
und das Glas ist kaputt.
**I would like my glasses repaired. I dropped
them yesterday and the lens is broken.**
Ich werde sehen, was ich für Sie tun kann.
Kommen Sie bitte morgen um elf zurück.
**I'll see what I can do for you. Come back
tomorrow at 11am.**

Grammar

Prepositions Governing The Accusative

The following prepositions are always followed by the **ACCUSATIVE** case:

für	-	for
um	-	at, round
durch	-	through
entlang	-	along
bis	-	until
ohne	-	without
gegen	-	against, towards (gegen die Wand - against the wall)
wider	-	against (wider meinen Willen - against my will)

e.g. Danke für Ihre Mühe - **thank you for your trouble**
   Gleich um die Ecke - **just round the corner**
   Durch den Tunnel - **through the tunnel**
   Die Straße entlang - **along the street**
   Ohne Versicherung - **without insurance (often used without an article)**

LASSEN

The verb lassen (to leave) when used together with another verb in the infinitive means to have something
done:
Ich muss diesen Photoapparat reparieren lassen - **I must get this camera repaired**
Einmal in zwei Monaten lasse ich mir die Haare schneiden - **I get my hair cut once every 2 months.**

Mini Test

1. Imagine you have lost your suitcase/bag at the airport. Describe it and everything inside it in German to an official.
2. Make a list in German of everything you must get done before going on holiday.

Foundation

In der Apotheke - At the Chemist's

Was ist los?

What is the matter?

Ich fühle mich nicht wohl. Ich bin erkältet. Haben Sie etwas dagegen?

I don't feel well. I've got a cold. Can you give me something for it?

Sie können Aspirin nehmen, und wir haben Hustenbonbons.

You can take aspirin and we have cough sweets.

Beim Arzt - At the Doctor's

Was fehlt Ihnen?

What is the matter with you?

Ich habe seit drei Tagen Fieber, und ich habe Kopfschmerzen.

I have had a temperature and a headache for 3 days.

Ich gebe Ihnen ein Rezept. Nehmen Sie diese Tabletten dreimal täglich nach dem Essen.

I'll give you a prescription. Take these tablets 3 times a day after meals.

Was haben Sie? **What is the matter?**

Mein Knie tut weh. **My knee hurts.**

Lassen Sie mich mal sehen...Tut das weh? Ja?

Tragen Sie diese Salbe auf. Sie ist rezeptfrei.

Und Sie müssen sich ausruhen.

Let me see ... Does that hurt? Yes? Use this cream. You don't need a prescription. And you must rest.

Vocabulary

der Körper	-	the body
das Gesicht	-	face
der Kopf	-	head
der Hals	-	throat
der Arm	-	arm
die Hand	-	hand
der Finger	-	finger
der Rücken	-	back
der Bauch / der Magen	-	stomach
das Bein	-	leg
das Knie	-	knee
der Fuß	-	foot
die Schulter	-	shoulder
die Zunge	-	tongue
das Auge/die Augen	-	eye/eyes
das Ohr/die Ohren	-	ears
die Nase	-	nose
der Mund	-	mouth
der Zahn/die Zähne	-	tooth/teeth
die Apotheke	-	chemist's
die Erkältung	-	cold
erkältet sein / einen Schnupfen haben	-	to have a cold
die Grippe	-	flu
Fieber haben	-	to have a fever, temperature
Durchfall	-	diarrhoea

Magenverstimmung	-	upset stomach
Kopfschmerzen	-	head ache
Magenschmerzen	-	stomach ache
Halsschmerzen	-	sore throat
mir ist heiß	-	I am hot
mir ist kalt	-	I am cold
mir ist übel/schlecht	-	I feel ill
mir ist schwindlig	-	I feel dizzy
das Rezept	-	prescription
rezeptfrei	-	not on prescription
die Bandage	-	bandage
die Salbe	-	cream
Tabletten	-	tablets
das Medikament	-	medicine
der Wespenstich	-	wasp sting
Ich habe Husten	-	I have a cough
der Hustenbonbon	-	cough sweet
die Seekrankheit	-	sea sickness
der Sonnenbrand	-	sunburn
der Gipsverband	-	plaster cast
das Hansaplast	-	elastoplast
die Spritze	-	injection
die Sprechstunden	-	consulting hours
allergisch gegen	-	allergic to
Heuschnupfen	-	hay fever

Higher

Beim Arzt - At the Doctor's

Guten Morgen. Wie kann ich Ihnen behilflich sein?

Good morning. How can I help you?

Guten Morgen Herr Doktor. Der Fuß tut mir unheimlich weh.

Good morning Doctor. My foot hurts dreadfully.

Lassen Sie mich mal sehen.. ..Ja, Sie haben sich den Fuß verrenkt. Sie dürfen nicht mit dem Fuß auftreten, und Sie müssen ins Krankenhaus - Sie brauchen einen Gipsverband.

Let me see ... yes, you have dislocated your foot. You must not put your weight on your foot and you will have to go to hospital - you need a plaster cast.

Wie waren die Ferien? **How were your holidays?**

Furchtbar ! Am ersten Tag hat mich eine Wespe gestochen. Das hat weh getan, und ich musste eine Salbe kaufen. Am nächsten Tag hatte ich Magenschmerzen und Durchfall, und ich musste im Bett bleiben, und am letzten Tag habe ich einen Sonnenbrand gekriegt. Nie wieder!

Awful! On the first day I got stung by a wasp. I was in a lot of pain and had to buy some cream. On the next day I had stomach ache and diarrhoea and had to stay in bed, and on the last day I got sunburn. Never again!

Grammar

Reflexive Pronouns In The Dative

The reflexive pronoun is usually in the accusative case - see reflexive verbs p.19.
However, there are a few verbs where the reflexive pronoun is in the DATIVE, and amongst these are reflexive verbs + a part of the body:

e.g. Ich wasche mich (accusative) - I have a wash BUT
     Ich wasche mir (dative) die Haare - I wash my hair
     Ich habe mir das Bein gebrochen - I have broken my leg
     Er hat sich den Fuß verstaucht - he has sprained his ankle

The reflexive pronouns in the dative are as follows:

NOMINATIVE		DATIVE
ich	-	mir
du	-	dir
er	-	sich
sie	-	sich
es	-	sich
wir	-	uns
ihr	-	euch
Sie/sie	-	sich

Mini Test

1. List as many parts of the body as you can in German in 30 seconds.
2. Imagine a conversation in a chemist's in German, in which you describe 3 ailments.
   What remedies could be offered?

Foundation

Bist du sportlich?
Are you sporty?
Ja, ich treibe gern Sport.
Yes, I enjoy sport.

Isst du gesund?
Do you eat healthily?
Ja, ich esse viel Obst und Gemüse und ich trinke sechs Glas Wasser pro Tag.
Yes, I eat lots of fruit and vegetables, and I drink 6 glasses of water a day.

Was machst du, um fit zu bleiben?
What do you do to keep fit?
Ich treibe oft Sport, und ich esse gesund.
I often play sports, and I eat healthily.

Was sollte man nicht essen?
What should one not eat?
Man sollte nicht zu viel Süßes essen oder zu viel Kaffee trinken.
One should not eat too many sweet things and one should not drink too much coffee.

Rauchst du?/trinkst du Alkohol?
Do you smoke?/drink alcohol?
Nein, ich rauche nie. Das ist ungesund.
Ab und zu trinke ich ein Bier.
No, I never smoke. It's bad for your health. I occasionally have a beer.

Wann gehst du ins Bett?
What time do you go to bed?
In der Woche gehe ich ziemlich früh ins Bett.
During the week I go to bed quite early.

Vocabulary

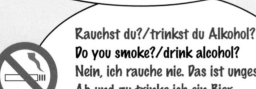

die Gesundheit	-	health	Drogen	-	drugs
gesund	-	healthy	gefährlich	-	dangerous
ungesund	-	unhealthy	das Risiko	-	risk
Sport treiben	-	to play sports	aus Neugier	-	out of curiosity
Obst	-	fruit	ekelhaft	-	disgusting
Gemüse	-	vegetables	ab und zu	-	from time to time
Süßigkeiten Bonbons	-	sweets	oft	-	often
			regelmäßig	-	regularly
Fett	-	fat (in food)	selten	-	rarely
das Fleisch	-	meat	früh	-	early
Vegetarier/Vegetarierin	-	vegetarian (m/f)	spät	-	late
vegetarisch essen	-	to be a vegetarian	Pickel	-	spots
Diät halten	-	to go on a diet	der Stress	-	stress
Kalorien verbrauchen	-	to use up calories	stressig	-	stressful
vermeiden	-	to avoid	müde	-	tired
versuchen	-	to try	deprimiert	-	depressed
rauchen	-	to smoke	Jugendprobleme	-	problems of adolescence
Zigaretten	-	cigarettes	fit und gesund bleiben	-	to remain fit and healthy
Alkohol	-	alcohol	sich entspannen	-	to relax

Higher

Was sind die Risiken, wenn man Drogen nimmt?
What are the risks of taking drugs?
Die Abhängigkeit, und für die, die spritzen, besteht auch das Risiko AIDS zu bekommen.
Dependancy, and for those who inject, the risk of AIDS.

Was bedeutet für dich "gesund essen"?
What does "eating healthily" mean for you?
Ich esse kein Fleisch und wenig Fett. Ich versuche, Süßigkeiten zu vermeiden und ich trinke keinen Alkohol.
I don't eat meat, and little fat. I try to avoid sweets and I don't drink alcohol.

Warum ist es wichtig, sich zu entspannen?
Und was machst du, um dich zu entspannen?
Why is it important to relax? And what do you do to relax?
Man muss sich Zeit für sich nehmen, sonst wird man unter Stress leiden. Um mich zu entspannen, höre ich Musik, oder ich telefoniere mit Freunden.
You have to have some time for yourself, otherwise you will suffer from stress. To relax, I listen to music or chat to friends on the telephone.

Warum rauchen und trinken deiner Meinung nach so viele Jugendliche?
In your opinion, why do so many young people smoke/drink?
Ich glaube, man macht das aus Neugier oder weil sie denken, sie sehen cool aus.
Out of curiosity I think, or because they think it looks cool.

Grammar

The Negative

The word NICHT is used to express NOT:
Ich rauche nicht - I do not smoke

The word KEIN is used with NOUNS to express the idea NOT ANY, NOT A, or NO:
Ich esse kein Fleisch - I don't eat meat
Ich trinke keinen Alkohol - I don't drink alcohol.
KEIN is declined in the same way as EIN.

Remember that NICHT + EIN = KEIN

NICHTS is used to express NOTHING:
Ich esse nichts zum Frühstück - I don't eat anything for breakfast.

Other negative expressions include:

nicht mehr	-	no longer	niemand	- nobody
nie	-	never	nirgendwo	- nowhere
noch nicht	-	not yet	gar nichts	- nothing at all
noch nie	-	never yet	weder....noch	- neither....nor

Mini Test

Give 5 tips to a German-speaking friend who needs to develop a healthier life style !

Foundation

Wie oft siehst du fern?
How often do you watch TV?
Ich sehe ungefähr eine Stunde pro Tag fern.
I watch approximately one hour of TV a day.

Was liest du zuerst
in der Zeitung/Zeitschrift?
**What do you read first of all in the
newspaper/magazine?**
Ich lese zuerst die Schlagzeilen, und dann
lese ich die Sportartikel.
**I read the headlines first of all, and then
I read the sports items.**

Was ist deine Lieblingssendung? Warum?
What is your favourite programme and why?
Meine Lieblingssendung ist "Animal Hospital",
weil ich Tiere mag.
**My favourite programme is "Animal Hospital"
because I like animals.**

Liest du oft Zeitung?
Do you often read a newspaper?
Ja, ich lese immer eine
Tageszeitung/nein ich lese lieber
eine Jugendzeitschrift, oder ich
lese eine Wochenzeitung.
**Yes, I always read a daily
newspaper/no, I prefer to read
a teenage magazine or I read the
weekly paper.**

Hörst du gern Radio?
**Do you like listening
to the radio?**
Ja, wenn ich unterwegs
bin, oder wenn ich meine
Hausaufgaben mache.
**Yes, when I'm travelling
or when I'm doing
my homework.**

Hast du eine Lieblingsgruppe?/einen Lieblingssänger?/eine Lieblingssängerin?
Do you have a favourite group?/a favourite male singer?/a favourite female singer?
Meine Lieblingsgruppe ist U2, weil sie unheimlich gut im Konzert ist.
Ich habe keinen Lieblingssänger/keine Lieblingssängerin.
**My favourite group is U2 because they are so good in concert.
I don't have a favourite singer.**

Vocabulary

das Fernsehen	- television		die Werbung	- advertising
das Satellitenfernsehen	- satellite television		die Anzeige	- advert
das Kabelfernsehen	- cable television		die Reklame	- advertising, advert
die Sendung	- programme		die Nachrichten	- news
das Programm	- channel, programme		der Bericht	- report
der Fernsehkanal/kanäle	- TV channel/channels		die Wettervorhersage	- weather forecast
das Radio	- radio		der Computer	- computer
die Zeitung	- newspaper		der Bildschirm	- screen
die Tageszeitung	- daily paper		der Camcorder	- camcorder
die Wochenzeitung	- weekly paper		die Auswahl	- choice
die Zeitschrift	- magazine		sich interessieren für	- to be interested in
die Presse	- press		sich informieren über	- to learn about, to find out about
die Schlagzeilen	- headlines		Lieblings + noun	- favourite ...

Higher

Wie findest du Kabelfernsehen? What do you think of cable TV?
Obwohl man mehr Auswahl hat, gibt es so viele Wiederholungen, dass man oft nichts zum Ansehen finden kann.
Although there is a greater choice, there are so many repeats that you often can't find anything to watch.

Findest du Werbung eine gute Sache? Do you think advertising is a good thing?
Einige Reklamen können ganz witzig und unterhaltsam sein, aber ich finde, dass viele Leute sich von der Werbung beeinflussen lassen und sie kaufen Sachen, die sie eigentlich nicht brauchen.
Some adverts can be quite funny and entertaining, but I think a lot of people are influenced by advertising, and buy things which they don't actually need.

Was sind die Vor-und Nachteile der neuesten Technologie?
What are the advantages and disadvantages of the latest technology?
Ich glaube, dass es heutzutage nicht mehr möglich ist, ohne Computer zu arbeiten. Man kann viel Zeit sparen, wenn man einen Computer hat. Auf der anderen Seite können Computer Arbeitsplätze gefährden, und man sollte nicht zu viel Zeit vor dem Computer sitzen, weil es schlecht für die Augen ist.
I don't think it is possible to work without computers today. You can save yourself a lot of time if you have a computer. On the other hand, computers can threaten jobs, and one should not spend too much time in front of a computer because it is bad for your eyes.

Grammar

Conjunctions

Conjunctions are words which join two parts of a sentence together e.g. "and", "or", "but".

There are five conjunctions in German which do NOT AFFECT WORD ORDER AT ALL. They are:
und - and, oder - or, aber - but, denn - because, sondern - but (on the other hand)

e.g. Wir haben einen Computer zu Hause, und ich habe beim Arbeitspraktikum mit Computern gearbeitet.
We have a computer at home and I used computers whilst on work experience.

There are other conjunctions which send the verb to the end of the sentence/clause; some of the most common are:

als	when, as	wenn	when, if
bis	until	weil	because
dass	that	damit	in order that
ob	whether, if	falls	in case, if
obwohl	although	bevor	before
während	while	nachdem	after
		seitdem	since

e.g. Ich glaube, dass einige Reklamen ganz witzig sind - I think that some adverts are quite funny.
Man kann viel Zeit sparen, wenn man einen Computer hat - You can save yourself a lot of time if you have a computer.
Ich höre Radio, während ich meine Hausaufgaben mache - I listen to the radio whilst doing my homework.

The clause beginning with the conjunction is called the SUBORDINATE CLAUSE;
the other part of the sentence, the MAIN CLAUSE, can stand alone, whereas the subordinate clause cannot.

Foundation

Welche Probleme gibt es in deiner Gegend?
What problems are there in your area?
Es gibt viel Verkehr auf der Straße, und das verpestet die Luft.
There is a lot of traffic on the roads and that pollutes the air.

Bist du umweltfreundlich?
Was tust du für die Umwelt?
Are you environmentally friendly?
What do you do to help the environment?
Ja, ich bin ziemlich umweltfreundlich.
Ich recycle Glas, Papier und Metall.
Ich benutze eine Stofftasche
statt einer Plastiktüte, wenn
ich einkaufen gehe.
Yes, I'm fairly
environmentally friendly.
I recycle glass, paper
and metal. I use a cloth bag
when I go shopping instead
of a plastic carrier bag.

Wie könnte man deine
Stadt/dein Dorf verbessern?
How could one improve your
town/village?
Wir brauchen eine neue Klinik
und etwas für die Jugendlichen.
We need a new clinic and
something for young people.

Wie behindertenfreundlich
ist deine Stadt?
What are the facilities for
the disabled like in your town?
Nicht besonders. Wegen der
engen Fußwege, ist es schwierig
für Rollstuhlfahrer, durch die
Stadt zu kommen.
Not especially good. Because of
the narrow pavements it is
difficult for wheelchair users
to get through town.

Was ist das größte Problem in der Gegend?
What is the biggest problem in the region?
Meiner Meinung nach sind es die Obdachlosen.
Während der Nacht schlafen viele draußen.
In my opinion it is the homeless. During the
night lots of people sleep outdoors.

Vocabulary

die Umwelt	-	the environment	das Treibhauseffekt -	the greenhouse effect
der Umweltschutz	-	protection of the environment	die Arbeitslosigkeit -	unemployment
die Umweltverschmutzung	-	pollution	die Armut -	poverty
umweltfreundlich	-	environmentally friendly	die Kriminalität -	crime
verpesten	-	to pollute	das Verbrechen -	crime
die Luft	-	the air	Gesellschaftsprobleme -	social problems
der Verkehr	-	traffic	die Einrichtungen für Behinderte -	facilities for the disabled
der Müll	-	rubbish	lösen -	to solve
der Abfall	-	rubbish	verderben -	to spoil
die Vorteile	-	advantages	schützen -	to protect
die Nachteile	-	disadvantages	verbessern -	to improve
das Recyceln	-	recycling	verschwenden -	to waste
recyceln	-	to recycle	unterstützen -	to support
die Obdachlosen	-	the homeless	sich Sorgen machen über -	to worry about
die Ozonschicht	-	the ozone layer	sich kümmern um -	to concern oneself with
das Ozonloch	-	the hole in the ozone layer	meiner Meinung nach -	in my opinion

Higher

> Was sind Deiner Meinung nach, die größten Gesellschaftsprobleme von heute?
> **In your opinion, what are the biggest social problems of today?**
> Die Armut, die Arbeitslosigkeit und die Kriminalität. Trotz der Fortschritte des zwanzigsten Jahrhunderts bleiben diese Probleme. Die Regierung muss etwas machen, um sie zu lösen.
> **Poverty, unemployment and crime. Despite the advances of the twentieth century these problems still remain. The Government must do something to solve them.**

> Und die Umwelt?
> Machst du dir darüber Sorgen?
> **And the environment? Do you worry about that?**
> Ich glaube, alle müssen etwas machen, um die Umwelt zu schützen, um unserer Kinder willen, damit sie unseren Planeten in der Zukunft genießen können.
> **I think everyone must do something to protect the environment, for the sake of our children, so that they can enjoy our planet in the future.**

SAVE OUR PLANET

HELP THE THIRD WORLD NOW!

> Sollten wir uns um die Probleme der dritten Welt kümmern?
> **Should we concern ourselves with the problems of the Third World?**
> Es wäre sehr egoistisch, wenn wir nichts machten, um diesen Menschen zu helfen. Es gibt viele Projekte und Organisationen, die man unterstützen kann.
> **It would be very selfish if we did nothing to help these people. There are lots of projects and organisations that one can support.**

Grammar

Prepositions Governing The Genitive

The following prepositions are always followed by the genitive:

(an)statt - **instead of**	außerhalb - **outside**	während - **during**
trotz - **in spite of**	innerhalb - **inside**	
wegen - **on account of, because of**	um.....willen* - **for the sake of**	

e.g. Trotz des schlechten Wetters, schlafen viele Leute draußen - **in spite of the cold weather, many people sleep outside**
Statt eines neuen Kinos, sollte man die Einrichtungen für Behinderte verbessern - **instead of a new cinema, the facilites for disabled should be improved.**
Während des Winters sind die Nächte sehr kalt - **during the winter the nights are very cold**
Um unserer Kinder willen müssen wir was tun - **for the sake of our children we must do something**
Außerhalb der Stadtmitte - **outside the town centre**

* Note: um meinetwegen, seinetwegen - **for my sake, for his sake**

Verbs Followed By The Dative

A number of verbs in German are always followed by the **DATIVE**. Some of the most common are:

helfen - **to help**	glauben - **to believe**
begegnen - **to meet**	danken - **to thank**
folgen - **to follow**	

Also gelingen **and** gefallen - **see impersonal verbs page 53.**

e.g. wir müssen diesen Menschen helfen - **we have to help these people**
ich glaube ihm nicht - **I don't believe him**   folgen Sie mir bitte - **please follow me.**

You will find the following phrases useful when conversing in German:

Wie bitte?	-	pardon, sorry?
Ich verstehe nicht (ganz)	-	I don't (quite) understand
Können Sie/ kannst du bitte langsamer sprechen?	-	Can you speak more slowly please?
Können Sie/kannst du das bitte wiederholen?	-	Can you repeat that please?
Können Sie/kannst du das bitte buchstabieren?	-	Can you spell that please?
Wie schreibt man das?	-	How do you spell that?
Ich kann ein bisschen/ganz gut/ gut/sehr gut/fließend Deutsch	-	I can speak German a little/quite well/ well/very well/fluently
Es steht hier ...	-	It says here ...
Es steht nicht hier	-	It doesn't say (i.e. the information is not given)
Das weiß ich nicht	-	I don't know
Ich bin nicht ganz sicher	-	I'm not quite sure
Was bedeutet das?	-	What does that mean?
Wie sagt man das auf Englisch?	-	How do you say that in English?
Wie sagt man ... auf Deutsch?	-	How do you say ... in German?
Ich habe das Wort für ... vergessen	-	I've forgotten the word for ...
Entschuldigen Sie/entschuldige bitte ...	-	excuse me please ...
Es tut mir Leid	-	I'm sorry
Guten Morgen	-	Good Morning
Guten Tag	-	Hello
Guten Abend	-	Good Evening
Gute Nacht	-	Goodnight
Auf Wiedersehen	-	Goodbye
Auf Wiederhören	-	Goodbye (on the telephone)
Hallo	-	Hello, hi
Tschüss	-	bye
Bis bald	-	See you soon
Wie geht's?	-	How are you?
Gut danke	-	fine, thanks
Danke/danke schön/danke sehr/vielen Dank	-	thank you
bitte/bitte schön/bitte sehr/gern geschehen	-	don't mention it, you're welcome
bitte	-	please
Einen Moment/einen Augenblick bitte	-	Just a moment please
Ich glaube, (dass)	-	I think (that)

Here are some common German instructions used in examination papers:

Beantworte die Fragen	-	answer the questions
Begrüße	-	greet
Beispiel	-	example
Beschreibe	-	describe
Erkläre	-	explain
Erzähle	-	tell
Falsch	-	false
Finde	-	find
Frage	-	ask
Fülle ... aus	-	fill in
Gib Information über	-	give information about
Hake ... an	-	tick
Hör (gut) zu	-	listen (carefully)
Kreuze ... an	-	put a cross
Lies den Artikel	-	read the article
Lies den Text und füll die Lücken aus	-	read the text and fill in the gaps
Mache Notizen	-	make notes
Nimm Abschied von ...	-	say Goodbye to ...
Ordne die Sätze/Bilder	-	put the sentences/pictures in the correct order
Richtig	-	true, correct
Sag	-	say
Sag deine Meinung über	-	give (i.e. say) your opinion about
Schau ... an	-	look at
Schreib an deinen Brieffreund/deine Brieffreundin	-	write to your penfreind (m/f)
Schreib die richtige(n) Nummer(n)	-	write the correct number(s)
Schreib die richtigen Namen neben die Bilder hin	-	write the correct names next to the pictures
Schreib einen Bericht über	-	write a report about
Schreib einen Brief an	-	write a letter to
Sieh ... an	-	look at
Stell Fragen über	-	ask questions about
Tabelle	-	table, grid
Unterstreiche	-	underline
Vergleiche	-	compare
Wähle	-	choose
Was bedeuten diese Symbole?	-	what do these symbols mean?
Was passt zusammen?	-	what goes together?
Zeichne mit einem X	-	mark with a X

Notes

The exact format of the oral examination will vary from one examination board to another, but you can expect to encounter AT LEAST the first two types of task listed below:

a) A role play situation in which you might find yourself whilst visiting a German-speaking country e.g. café, bank, shopping, or discussing something with a German-speaking penfriend. The number of role plays will depend on the particular examination board and/or your level of entry.

b) A conversation about yourself, your family, your hobbies and interests, past and future holidays etc in either a general conversation or an interview situation.

c) A narrative task in the past tense, using a series of visual prompts.

d) A short presentation on a topic of interest to you, taken from the GCSE topic areas, and which may then be developed further in the following conversation.

Role Play

You are unlikely to know which role play situation(s) you will be given before the examination, but if you have revised well and learnt some stock phrases for each topic area you should be able to cope easily. You will be given some preparation time before the start of your oral examination, and you may be allowed to make notes (but you will not be able to take your notes into the examination room).

Example: Im Hotel

You have arrived at a German hotel. You would like rooms for your family. The examiner will play the part of the receptionist and will speak first. (i)

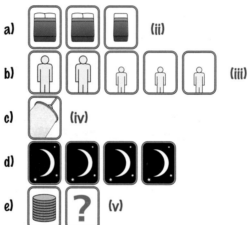

Role Play Notes

(i) Make sure you know where the situation is taking place and what your role is (in hotel reception, as a tourist seeking accommodation). Also make sure you know what the teacher's/examiner's role is, and whether to address him/her as 'du' or 'Sie' (here - hotel receptionist - use the polite 'Sie' form of address). Check who speaks first.

(ii) The visuals are designed to give you an idea of what to say; study them carefully.

(iii) Remember that you are taking part in a conversation and must respond to what the teacher/examiner says and not simply carry out the tasks as if he/she were not there!

(iv) If you cannot manage the whole phrase, say what you can - even if it is just one or two words. 'Dusche' is a key word here so even that one word will earn you a mark.

(v) Make sure you revise question forms.

Don't give up! Even if you are struggling with a particular role play, always try to finish it off. Remember that marks are awarded for relevant communication.

Some role plays contain an element of unpredictability - be aware of this so that you are not caught off guard.

Conversation / Interview

The conversation topics are normally: Self and Others, Home and Daily Routine, Hobbies and Interests, Education and Career, Geographical Surroundings and Holidays and Tourism. All these topics have been covered in this guide.

Example: You have an interview
for the following office job in Austria :

You are asked questions about the following: (i)

Interviewfragen: Name/Alter (ii)
                          Familie
                          Schule/Fächer (iii)
                          Nächstes Jahr (iv)
                          Hobbys und Interessen (v)
                          Dieser Job - warum? (vi)

GESUCHT
Aushilfe für generelle Büroarbeit
Drei Monate (Juni bis August)
Deutsch und Englischkenntnisse nötig
gut bezahlt

Conversation / Interview Notes

(i)   Again, make sure you know what you have to do. As this is a formal interview setting, you will address the teacher/examiner as 'Sie'.

(ii)   Your teacher/examiner will prompt you with a question; try and give as much detail as possible, and take the initiative to move on and talk about your family - the more you say the better.

(iii) If you find that you are struggling at a particular point, the teacher/examiner will be aware of this and will intervene with another question to help you move on.

(iv)   This is where you will be expected to bring in a different tense (although you may already have done so). Remember that you do not have to tell the truth - no-one will check!

(v)   Aim to use a variety of vocabulary and different constructions throughout. Try hard with your German accent and intonation - all these things will help to improve your marks.

(vi)   Refer back to the job advert in order to explain why you want this post - they have provided you with some ideas - make use of them! ALWAYS BE PREPARED FOR THE 'WARUM' QUESTION BY BEING ABLE TO JUSTIFY YOUR RESPONSES, FEELINGS AND OPINIONS.

Remember to keep calm and don't rush your answers. Your teacher/examiner will always help you out if you get stuck.

Narrative Task
A thorough knowledge of the past tenses (perfect, imperfect, even possibly pluperfect) is required for this type of task. Make good use of the visual clues and vocabulary provided, although you do not have to adhere rigidly to everything given. This is not a monologue - you will still be expected to respond to questions and comments from your teacher/examiner.

Presentation
It makes sense to choose a topic which interests you and about which you have plenty to say - a special hobby or interest, or an unforgettable holiday for example. Make sure the presentation title allows you enough scope to use a wide range of vocabulary and structure, and a variety of tenses. There will be a follow-up discussion so it is advisable to spend some time thinking about the possible questions your teacher/examiner may ask.

The best preparation for this part of the GCSE assessment is to listen to as much spoken German as you can:

- Radio and/or satellite television.

- A visit to Germany/a German-speaking country.

- Exchanging cassettes with a German penfriend.

- The use of listening materials from school.

Together with this of course you must have a sound base of German vocabulary across the topic areas. At Foundation level you can expect to hear announcements, instructions, requests, dialogues, short news items. At Higher level you can expect to hear longer and more complex passages. Here are some points to bear in mind for your listening exam :

- Before the examination, familiarise yourself with instructions in German (see page 71).

- At the start of the examination, look carefully at any examples given and always read the questions in advance so you know what you are listening out for:
  e.g. Das Hotel ist ...
    a) in der Stadtmitte
    b) außerhalb der Stadt
    c) neben dem Freizeitzentrum

You will have time to study the three alternatives before hearing:

Es gibt hier so viel zu sehen und zu machen. Am ersten Tag haben wir die Altstadt besucht und gestern haben wir Squash im Freizeitzentrum gespielt. <u>Unser Hotel</u> ist sehr modern und bequem und <u>liegt im Stadtzentrum</u>.

Only the information underlined is required to answer the question. The rest can be ignored. Notice that although you hear some information about the leisure centre, this is not required to answer the question - wait until you have heard everything before you make your decision.

- Do not worry, particularly at Higher level, if you don't understand every single word. Concentrate on listening out for the information required by the question

- Check how many marks a question is worth - if the whole question is worth 11 marks that tells you that you need to tick 11 boxes or provide 11 pieces of information

- If asked to tick 3 boxes, do not tick more than 3 in the hope that the correct 3 will be among them! You will be penalised for doing this.

- Similarly, do not leave a question unanswered. There are no marks awarded for blank spaces, but an intelligent guess may gain you marks.

- Remember that you will hear each item more than once, and that you can make notes throughout. Check if answers have to be written in German or English and remember that you do not have to write in full sentences, and that German answers will not be marked for accuracy, only comprehension.

The reading assessment is based on a range of written texts, varying in length and complexity from e.g. a short public notice to a newspaper or magazine article.
Much of the advice for the listening examination is also relevant here.

- Read the titles and the questions carefully. They often provide a helpful context.
- Scan the text for information related to the question, then go back to the question - what exactly is wanted?
- Sometimes, especially with longer items, the trick is to understand the gist, the general idea and not every single word. In such cases, it is a matter of finding the relevant piece of information and you are not expected or required to understand everything.
- Sometimes the answer hinges on one little word, which you must be careful not to overlook :
  e.g. Consider these two sentences:

Ich habe alle Fächer gern, besonders Englisch - I like all subjects ESPECIALLY English.

Ich habe alle Fächer gern außer Englisch - I like all subjects EXCEPT English.

'Besonders' and 'außer' both play a crucial role in the understanding of the sentence. Make sure your revision includes a list of these short but very important words!

- Sometimes you will be able to deduce meaning from context:

Die meisten alten Tannen im Schwarzwald sind nicht mehr zu retten, aber die jungen Bäume hofft man
zu schützen ...

    The words 'Wald' and 'Bäume' will hopefully lead you to recognise that 'Tannen' are a type of tree, which may help you make sense of the passage; you would not be expected however to know that 'Tannen' are fir trees.

    It may be useful to break down compound nouns to understand the meaning:

e.g. Klassenfahrt contains Klasse (class) and Fahrt (journey, trip) =
    a class, or school trip
    Schreibwaren-schreiben is to write, Waren are goods, merchandise, therefore
    Schreibwaren = stationary.

- Use clues offered by the language and grammar of the text; you will need to be able to recognise different tenses and verb forms, singular and plural nouns, which gender is required etc.
  e.g. the following words are provided for this gap-filling exercise:

| der | dem | die | alt | älteren | älter | Haus | Tradition | sehe | verstehen | spielt |

a) Meine _____ Brüder arbeiten beide im Ausland. (Adjective, nominative, plural required).
b) Das ist eine alte _____ . (Noun, nominative, feminine required).
c) Das kann man gut _____ . (Verb, infinitive, following modal verb 'kann')
d) Er kommt mit _____ Bus. (Definite article, dative following 'mit', masculine - Bus)

For specific details of the listening and reading assessments you will need to check the requirements of your own syllabus.

Foundation

At Foundation level, you may be required to write out a list, fill in a form, write a note, postcard or letter.

A FORM

e.g. 1 - Sie haben etwas verloren und sind jetzt im Fundbüro. Füllen Sie dieses Formular aus! (i)

		marks
Datum (ii)	den achten April	(1)
Name/Vorname (iii)	Robinson, Charlotte	(2)
Adresse	Hotel Adler, Bahnhofstraße 1	(1)
Was?	eine Handtasche	(1)
Beschreibung (iv)	klein, braun, aus Leder	(3)
Wo? (v)	am Busbahnhof	(2)

Notes

(i)   As always, make sure you understand the instructions. Notice that it has been left up to you to decide what you have lost.

(ii) Try to include some German rather than just putting the date in numbers.

(iii) Make sure you get your names the right way round! (Name = surname)

(iv) Check how many marks are available so you know how many details to provide.

(v)   Include a preposition - 'am Busbahnhof'.

A POSTCARD

e.g. 2 - Du bist auf Urlaub. Schreib eine Postkarte an deinen Brieffreund/deine Brieffreundin!
Schreib
a) wo du bist

b) wie das Wetter ist

c) wo du wohnst

d) was du da machst

e) wie lange du da bleibst (i)

Schreib ungefähr 30 Wörter (ii)

Liebe Brita,
ich bin auf Urlaub in Wales. Das Wetter ist sonnig und warm. Wir wohnen in einem Hotel.
Jeden Tag gehe ich schwimmen und spiele Tennis. Wir bleiben zwei Wochen.

Viele Grüße
Pam (iii)

(29 words, not including Liebe/viele Grüße)

Notes

(i)   Once you have decided what you need to do, have a look at the instructions once again to see if there are any phrases you can use. You will need to make some changes e.g. to verb endings - du bleibst - wir bleiben

(ii) Notice how many words you need to write. You will be penalised if your work is too long or too short.

(iii) Always check your work. A check list should include: spellings, genders, tenses and appropriate endings for cases, adjectives, verbs.

Foundation / Higher

You may be required to write a letter, either formal or informal at both Foundation and Higher level.

A LETTER TO A FRIEND

e.g. 1 - Dein deutscher Brieffreund/deine deutsche Brieffreundin kommt nächsten Monat auf Besuch. Schreib ihm/ihr und sage, was für Pläne du hast und frage ihn/sie, was er/sie gern machen möchte. (i)

Dein Brief soll wie ein richtiger Brief beginnen und enden.
Schreib 100 bis 120 Wörter

Dunstable, den 23. Juni

Lieber Peter, (ii)

Danke für Deinen letzten Brief (iii). Ich mache schon Pläne für Deinen Besuch. Meine Eltern und ich werden Dich vom Flughafen abholen, und dann werden wir das Wochenende in London verbringen (iv). Wir werden die Sehenswürdigkeiten besichtigen, und wir hoffen, ein Musical zu sehen (v). Wir werden auch andere Ausflüge machen - möchtest Du etwas Bestimmtes sehen?

Zu Hause können wir mit dem Computer spielen. Magst Du gern Computerspiele? (vi)

Wir werden schwimmen gehen und ins Kino gehen. Hast Du schon den neuen James Bond Film gesehen?

Letztes Wochenende habe ich Karten für ein Fußballspiel während Deines Aufenthalts besorgt (vii); wir können zusammen hingehen.

Ich freue mich auf Deinen Besuch! Bis bald! (viii)

Dein

Daniel　　　　　(106 words not including letter beginning or ending)

Notes

(i)　Decide whether the letter is formal or informal. As this is a letter to a penfriend, the 'du' form of address is used. Decide also which tense(s) you will need to use.

(ii)　Make sure you have the appropriate beginning and ending to your letter: Lieber/liebe (m/f) and Dein/Deine (m/f) at the end. Remember that you don't need your full address - just the town/village from where you are writing and the date.

(iii)　You need a suitable opening sentence for your letter.

(iv)　Check your word order, especially when using a construction such as werden + infinitive.

(v)　Try to include a zu + infinitive construction.

(vi)　Ask questions; they add variety and make for genuine communication.

(vii)　Try to include a variety of tenses, but remember to keep it relevant to the task set.

(viii)　Finish off with an appropriate ending. Check that your letter is the right length and provide a word count. Check work thoroughly (see no.(iii) page 76).

Higher

A FORMAL LETTER

e.g. 1 - Du warst neulich mit deiner Familie in einem Hotel in Österreich. Ihr habt dort viele Probleme gehabt. Schreib einen Brief an das Hotel. Schreib 100 bis 120 Wörter.

Adresse des Hotels - Hotel zum roten Löwen
Hauptstraße
Innsbruck

James Ashton

42 Kings Road

Manchester

den 8. September

Sehr geehrte Damen und Herren, (i)

Meine Familie und ich waren (ii) neulich vom 20. Bis 31. August, in Ihrem Hotel und wir waren mit unserem Aufenthalt gar (iii) nicht zufrieden.

Erstens (iv) war die Empfangsdame sehr unhöflich bei unserer Ankunft. Zweitens war das Schlafzimmer meiner Eltern im zweiten Stock, und der Fahrstuhl war außer Betrieb. Niemand hat uns mit den Koffern geholfen. Drittens war das Waschbecken in meinem Zimmer schmutzig, und die Dusche funktionierte nicht. Der Manager war nicht sehr hilfreich, und hat uns (v) nur angelächelt, als wir uns beschwert haben.

Ich muss auch mitteilen, dass (vi) es keine Reservierung für uns gab, obwohl (vi) ich schon letzten März telefonisch und schriftlich reserviert hatte. (vii)

Ich erwarte in naher Zukunft eine Erklärung von Ihnen.

Hochachtungsvoll,

Ihr

James Ashton   (110 words, not including letter beginning or ending)

Notes

(i)   As this is a formal letter of complaint you will need to give your full address, as you expect a reply. Note the formal letter beginning and ending.

(ii)   Be careful with verb endings in instances such as these - "my family and I" = "we".

(iii)   Note how a little word like 'gar' (not at all) can stress your dissatisfaction with your stay.

(iv)   Note the use of 'erstens', 'zweitens' etc - useful when listing complaints.

(v)   The use of pronouns shows that you can manipulate the language.

(vi)   Note the use of subordinating conjunctions which send the verb to the end of the sentence/clause.

(vii) As well as the perfect and imperfect tenses, a pluperfect has been introduced here.

Higher

AN ARTICLE/ESSAY

e.g. 1 - Schreib einen Artikel über das englische und das deutsche Schulsystem für eine deutsche Schulzeitschrift. Schreib 150 Wörter. (i)

Ich besuche eine Gesamtschule in Oxford. Die Schule beginnt um Viertel vor neun, das ist etwas später als in Deutschland. Der Schultag ist auch länger (ii) hier in England; bei uns ist die Schule um vier Uhr aus. Wir müssen eine Uniform tragen, die (iii) sehr hässlich ist. Ich trage eine weiße Bluse, eine blaue Krawatte mit gelben Streifen (iv) und einen blauen Rock. Ich finde meine Uniform unbequem - ich würde lieber ein Sweatshirt und eine Hose tragen (v). In der Mittagspause bleibe ich in der Schule und esse in der Kantine, wo man gesund und billig essen kann.

Obwohl (vi) man in Deutschland sitzenbleiben muss, wenn (vi) man immer schlechte Noten bekommt, ziehe ich das deutsche Schulsystem vor - ich finde das besser, wenn die Schule um eins aus ist, dann hat man den Nachmittag frei, und man kann Sport treiben oder Hausaufgaben machen, statt das am Abend zu machen, wenn man müde ist. (vii)

149 Wörter

Notes

(i) You need to think carefully about layout and structure for an article such as this - plan carefully before you start to write.

(ii) Use comparisons, rather than just a simple adjective to add variety and show greater command of the language.

(iii) Try to bring in a relative pronoun to link your sentences and make them more complex; remember that it will send the verb to the end of the sentence/clause.

(iv) Correct use of adjective endings and cases shows a good command of the language and rules of grammar.

(v) Introduce a conditional if possible.

(vi) Once again, subordinating conjunctions will provide examples of more complex language.

(vii) Make sure you always support your opinions with a reason why. If you have a title which asks you to discuss the pros and cons of something, or as here, to consider two different systems try to give a balanced account.

Even though dictionaries are not allowed in examinations, it is still very important that you are able to use a German-English/English-German dictionary for homework and independent study, and indeed for the preparation of coursework.

You need to be aware of the pitfalls of using a bilingual dictionary. Your teacher will have given you advice on how to use a dictionary effectively, but it is worth bearing the following points in mind:

- When alternative German words are offered in your dictionary, check each one in the German-English section to find the one with the correct meaning:

- e.g. English 'lead' - do you want ...
      ... Blei nt
      ... Graphit nt
      ... Spitzenposition f
      ... Führung f
      ... Vorsprung m
      ... führen vt
      ... anführen vt
      ... vorangehen vi ?!

- Be aware that the different structures of German and English do not allow for word to word translation. You need a sound understanding of the rules of grammar and sentence structure.

- You need to understand dictionary abbreviations:

  e.g.
m	-	masculine
f	-	feminine
nt	-	neuter
vt sep	-	verb, transitive, separable
vi aux sein	-	verb, intransitive, auxiliary verb in the perfect tense is sein

  and also instructions:

  e.g.   siehe auch ...   -   see also ...

- Remember that verbs are given in the infinitive e.g.

  spielen   -   to play

  And that you may well need to change the verb ending and indeed choose the correct tense for your own use:

er spielt	-	he plays, is playing
wir haben Fußball gespielt	-	we played, did play football

- Similarly, you may need to add an appropriate ending to an adjective you find in the dictionary, e.g.

frech	-	cheeky
sie ist ein freches Mädchen	-	she is a cheeky girl

NOUNS

All nouns in German are written with a capital letter. German nouns are either masculine (der), feminine (die) or neuter (das). This is known as the GENDER of a noun. When you look a word up in a dictionary, an 'm' following the noun indicates that it is masculine, an 'f' that it is feminine and 'nt' that it is neuter.

e.g.

Man - Mann (m)

Woman - Frau (f)

Baby - Baby (nt)

PLURAL NOUNS

In the plural, all genders become 'die' in German. Unlike English, very few nouns in German add an 's' in the plural. Although there are some rules governing plurals, it is best to learn plurals along with the noun itself and its gender.

Plurals are indicated in a dictionary in bold print following the noun:

e.g.

Bruder m, -s (genitive ending) , - ¨ (plural)

Schwester f, -(no genitive ending), -n (plural)

Baby nt, -s (genitive ending), -s (plural)

CASES

The idea of the 4 cases in German can be difficult to understand at first because so little use is made of them in English. In order to understand cases you have to understand the structure of sentences:

The simplest sentence will contain only a subject and a verb:

e.g.   Ich esse - I (subject) eat (verb).

Now we introduce an object:

Ich esse einen Apfel - I eat an apple (direct object)

Now we bring in an indirect object:

Ich gebe meinem Bruder einen Apfel - I (subject) give (verb) an apple (direct object) to my brother (indirect object)

When dealing with direct and indirect objects, as in the above example, ask yourself WHAT am I giving? (What is the object I am giving? - an apple) and also TO WHOM am I giving it? (To my brother. Indirect objects usually occur with verbs like to give, to show, and in English often have the word 'to' in front of them.)

And finally:

Das ist der Apfel meines Bruders - It's my brother's apple (the apple of my brother).

This case denotes POSSESSION.

The four cases in German are:

THE NOMINATIVE CASE - Used for the SUBJECT of the verb, and is the case used in vocabulary lists, because it clearly denotes gender.

THE ACCUSATIVE CASE - Used for the DIRECT OBJECT of the verb, and after certain prepositions.

THE GENITIVE CASE - Used to denote OWNERSHIP or POSSESSION, and after certain prepositions.

THE DATIVE CASE - Used for the INDIRECT OBJECT of the verb, also after certain prepositions and after certain verbs

DEFINITE ARTICLE

The definite article der, die, das is equivalent to the English 'the'. In German the definite article will change DEPENDING ON CASE AND GENDER. This is referred to as the DECLENSION of the definite article and is shown in the following table:

	masculine	feminine	neuter	plural
Nom.	der	die	das	die
Acc.	den	die	das	die
Gen.	des -(e)s	der	des -(e)s	der
Dat.	dem	der	dem	den -n

In the masculine and neuter forms of the genitive, an 's' is added to the singular noun. In nouns of one syllable, 'es' is often added. In the dative plural, an 'n' is added to the noun, unless it already ends in 'n'.

Some uses of the definite article in German:

- With days, months, and seasons:
  - am Dienstag (contracted form of an dem)   -   on Tuesday
  - im Mai (in dem)   -   in May
  - im Winter (in dem)   -   in Winter

- With feminine countries:
  - er fährt in die Schweiz   -   he is going to Switzerland

- With quantities, and frequency:
  - ein Euro, fünfzig Cents das Kilo   -   1 Euro 50 Cents a kilo
  - zweimal in der Woche   -   twice a week

- With parts of the body, and clothes where in English a possessive adjective would be used:
  - er hat sich das Bein gebrochen   -   he broke his leg
  - sie zog den Mantel aus   -   she took off her coat

Also in these examples where the definite article would not be used in English:
- er fährt in die Stadt   -   he is going into town
- sie fährt mit dem Zug   -   she is travelling by train
- morgen gehe ich in die Schule   -   I'm going to school tomorrow

INDEFINITE ARTICLE

The indefinite article, ein, eine is equivalent to the English 'a', 'an'.
It is declined in the following way:

	masculine	feminine	neuter	plural (of mein, kein etc)*
Nom.	ein	eine	ein	meine
Acc.	einen	eine	ein	meine
Gen.	eines -(e)s	einer	eines -(e)s	meiner
Dat.	einem	einer	einem	meinen -n

*Although 'ein' does not have a plural, 'kein' and the possessive adjectives mein, dein, sein, ihr, unser, euer, Ihr and ihr are all declined in the same way as 'ein', and they do have plural forms.

Remember that 'kein' is translated as 'not a', 'no' (+noun) or in the plural 'not any'.
The indefinite article is omitted in German when talking about nationalities and professions:
- Ich bin Engländer   -   I am an Englishman
- Er ist Tierarzt   -   he is a vet.

ADJECTIVES　See page 11

Remember that when an adjective is used on its own in German, it does not need an ending:

> Das Haus ist modern　-　The house is modern
> Die Schule ist groß　-　The school is big

When an adjective stands in front of the noun it is describing, an ending is required according to gender and case:

Northampton hat einen kleinen Bahnhof und ein großes Einkaufszentrum
Northampton has a small railway station and a large shopping centre

Sie fährt mit ihrer älteren Schwester auf Urlaub
She is going on holiday with her older sister

ADJECTIVE ENDINGS AFTER THE DEFINITE ARTICLE

After der, die, das and also dieser (this), jeder (each, every), jener (that), welcher (which), solcher (such), and alle (all) the adjective endings are as follows:

	masculine	feminine	neuter	plural
N	der kleine Mann	die kleine Frau	das kleine Kind	die kleinen Kinder
A	den kleinen Mann	die kleine Frau	das kleine Kind	die kleinen Kinder
G	des kleinen Mannes	der kleinen Frau	des kleinen Kindes	der kleinen Kinder
D	dem kleinen Mann	der kleinen Frau	dem kleinen Kind	den kleinen Kindern

These are actually very easy to remember as there are only two endings: -e and -en.

ADJECTIVE ENDINGS AFTER THE INDEFINITE ARTICLE

After ein, kein, and the possessive adjectives mein, dein, sein, ihr, unser, euer, Ihr and ihr the adjective endings are as follows:

	masculine	feminine	neuter	plural
N	ein alter Dom	eine alte Schule	ein altes Rathaus	keine alten Häuser
A	einen alten Dom	eine alte Schule	ein altes Rathaus	keine alten Häuser
G	eines alten Doms	einer alten Schule	eines alten Rathauses	keiner alten Häuser
D	einem alten Dom	einer alten Schule	einem alten Rathaus	keinen alten Häusern

ADJECTIVE ENDINGS WITHOUT AN ARTICLE

The following endings are used when there is NO definite or indefinite article in front of the adjective, and also following viele (many), wenige (few), mehrere (several), einige (some) and numbers (except ein):

	masculine	feminine	neuter	plural
N	kalter Kaffee	kalte Milch	kaltes Wasser	kalte Hände
A	kalten Kaffee	kalte Milch	kaltes Wasser	kalte Hände
G	kalten Kaffees	kalter Milch	kalten Wassers	kalter Hände
D	kaltem Kaffee	kalter Milch	kaltem Wasser	kalten Händen

Adjectives can be formed from the names of towns and cities, and are invariable i.e. do not change:

e.g.　　die Londoner Straßen　-　the streets of London
　　　　die Berliner Philharmonie　-　the Berlin Philharmonic Orchestra

ADJECTIVAL NOUNS

Almost all adjectives can be used as nouns. Write the adjective with a capital letter and decline in the same way as an adjective, using the above tables.

e.g.   der A<u>lte</u> ging langsam die Straße entlang - the old man walked slowly along the street

ein Al<u>ter</u> stand vor der Tür - an old man stood outside the door

Common adjectival nouns include:

der/die Verwandte - relative, relation (m/f)

der/die Fremde - stranger (m/f)

der/die Bekannte - aquaintance (m/f)

der/die Deutsche - German person (m/f)

THE COMPARATIVE AND SUPERLATIVE OF ADJECTIVES   See page 25

Other points to note:

the repeated comparative e.g. 'smaller and smaller' is translated in German by immer + comparative :

Die Nächte werden immer kälter - the nights are getting colder and colder

Adjectives ending in 'er' or 'el' drop the final 'e' in the comparative:

teuer   teu<u>rer</u> der/die/das teuerste - expensive, more expensive, most expensive

dunkel dunk<u>ler</u> der/die/das dunkelste - dark, darker, darkest

Note the use of the comparative:

Ich bin jünger als er - I am younger than he is

Er ist nicht so alt wie sie - he is not as old as she is

For comparing two equal things use:

(eben)so ... wie

er ist ebenso groß wie sein Bruder - he is as tall as his brother

POSSESSIVE ADJECTIVES   See page 11

Mein, dein, sein, ihr, unser, euer, Ihr **and** ihr

DEMONSTRATIVE ADJECTIVES   See page 45

Dieser (this), jener (that), jeder (each,every). Also solcher (such) - see below for use.

Demonstrative adjectives are declined like der, as follows:

	masculine	feminine	neuter	plural
N	dieser Mann	diese Frau	dieses Kind	diese Kinder
A	diesen Mann	diese Frau	dieses Kind	diese Kinder
G	dieses Mannes	dieser Frau	dieses Kindes	dieser Kinder
D	diesem Mann	dieser Frau	diesem Kind	diesen Kindern

Solcher (such) can be used in two ways:

ein solcher Mann - such a man (solcher has appropriate ending following ein)

solche Leute - such people (solche here declined like diese in the above table)

Note also: So ein kluges Kind - such a clever child

INTERROGATIVE ADJECTIVES

These are adjectives used when asking questions - welcher (which) and was für (what sort of).
See page 45 for welcher, which is declined like dieser.

Was für is invariable, but if followed by ein, the ein must be declined according to case and gender:

e.g.

was für eine Katze ist das? -	what kind of a cat is that? (nominative, feminine)
was für einen Hut trägt er? -	what kind of a hat is he wearing? (accusative, masculine)

ADVERBS   See page 57

Note these common adjectives which can be used as adverbs:

gut	-	good (adj), well (adv)
einfach	-	simple (adj), simply (adv)
langsam	-	slow (adj), slowly (adv)
schnell	-	quick (adj), quickly (adv)
spät	-	late (adj and adv)

Remember that adverbs are invariable - i.e. they do not change.
Note the following uses of hin and her:

Kommen Sie herein!	-	Come in!
Gehen Sie hinaus!	-	Go out!
Er ging die Treppe hinauf	-	he went upstairs
Er kam die Treppe herunter	-	he came downstairs

HER indicates motion TOWARDS the speaker.
HIN indicates motion AWAY FROM the speaker.

Adverbs are occasionally formed by adding - erweise to an adjective:

glücklicherweise	-	luckily
möglicherweise	-	possibly

COMPARATIVE AND SUPERLATIVE OF ADVERBS

The comparative of adverbs is formed in the same way as the comparative of adjectives, by adding 'er' on the end, and with some single syllable adverbs, an umlaut where appropriate. The superlative of adverbs is formed by using 'am' + ' -sten':

schnell	schneller	am schnellsten	- quick	quicker	most quickly
scharf	schärfer	am schärfsten	- sharp	more sharply	most sharply

Note these common irregular forms:

gut	besser	am besten	- well	better	best
früh	früher	am frühesten	- early	earlier/sooner	at the earliest
gern	lieber	am liebsten	- willingly	more willingly	most willingly

Remember that gern/lieber/am liebsten are used in the construction 'gern haben' - to like:

Ich habe Schach gern	-	I like chess
Ich habe Computerspiele lieber	-	I prefer computer games
Ich habe Sport am liebsten	-	I like sport best of all

COMPARATIVE AND SUPERLATIVE OF ADVERBS Continued from previous page

Or used with another verb:

Ich esse gern Obst	-	I like (eating) fruit
Ich esse lieber Nudeln	-	I prefer (to eat) pasta
Ich esse Pizza am liebsten	-	I like (eating) pizza best of all

Note also the following adverbial expressions:

meistens	-	mostly
spätestens	-	at the latest
wenigstens	-	at least
möglichst schnell/so schnell wie möglich	-	as quickly as possible

VERBS

There are two main types of verb in German, WEAK and STRONG.

- WEAK verbs follow a regular pattern of verb endings in the present and imperfect tenses.

- STRONG verbs have a change of vowel sound in the imperfect tense, and some strong verbs have special forms in the present tense.

THE PRESENT TENSE

- For the present tense of weak verbs, see page 9.
- For the present tense of strong verbs, see page 15.
- For the present tense of HABEN and SEIN, see page 9.

Verbs with a stem ending in 'd' or 't' add an extra 'e' before -st and -t endings, in order to make the word easier to say. The verb arbeiten illustrates this:

arbeiten - to work   present tense
ich arbeite   wir arbeiten
du arbeit<u>e</u>st   ihr arbeit<u>e</u>t
er/sie/es arbeit<u>e</u>t   Sie/sie arbeiten

This also happens in the imperfect and the past participle:

imperfect	-	ich arbeit<u>e</u>te
past participle	-	gearbeit<u>e</u>t

THE PERFECT TENSE

In the perfect tense, both weak and strong verbs are used with an auxiliary verb (either HABEN or SEIN) and a past participle.

The past participle of weak verbs usually begins with ge- and ends in -t.

The past participle of strong verbs usually begins with ge- and ends with -en, and sometimes has a vowel change to the stem vowel.

- For the perfect tense with haben as auxiliary verb, see page 29.

- For the perfect tense with sein as auxiliary verb, see page 33.

| **THE IMPERFECT TENSE** | See page 43 |

Of both weak and strong verbs.

| **THE PLUPERFECT TENSE** | See page 55 |

THE FUTURE TENSE

- For the use of the present tense in German to express the future, see page 15
- For the future tense using WERDEN, see page 27

| **THE CONDITIONAL TENSE** | See page 37 |

| **THE IMPERATIVE** | See page 39 |

MODAL VERBS

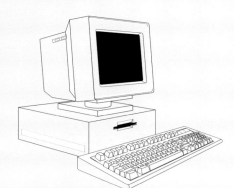

PRESENT TENSE - see page 31, page 35

IMPERFECT - see page 43

All six modal verbs are irregular. Here are the present tense forms:

	dürfen	können	mögen	müssen	sollen	wollen
ich	darf	kann	mag	muss	soll	will
du	darfst	kannst	magst	musst	sollst	willst
er/sie/es	darf	kann	mag	muss	soll	will
wir	dürfen	können	mögen	müssen	sollen	wollen
ihr	dürft	könnt	mögt	müsst	sollt	wollt
Sie/sie	dürfen	können	mögen	müssen	sollen	wollen

| **REFLEXIVE VERBS** | In the present and perfect tenses. See page 19 |

SEPARABLE AND INSEPARABLE VERBS

These are verbs which begin with a PREFIX (often a preposition). They can be weak or strong.
They fall into different categories depending on whether the prefix is separable or inseparable.
For examples of separable prefixes, see page 23.

Some very common separable prefixes are:
ab, an, auf, aus, bei, ein, fern, fort, her, hin, mit, vor, weiter, zu, zurück, zusammen

The inseparable prefixes are:
be-, ge-, er-, ver-, zer-, emp-, ent-, and miss. See also page 29.

Some prefixes are sometimes separable and sometimes inseparable, depending on the meaning of the verb.
These are:
durch, hinter, über, um, unter, voll, wider **and** wieder

e.g.
umsteigen (sep)	-	to change (trains etc)
Ich stieg in Köln um	-	I changed trains in Cologne
umarmen (insep)	-	to embrace
Er umarmte mich	-	he embraced me

A dictionary will tell you whether the verb is separable or inseparable - (sep) or (insep).

IMPERSONAL VERBS — See page 53

THE INFINITIVE

The infinitive of a verb indicates its meaning as follows:

> spielen   -   to play
> machen   -   to do, to make

Infinitives normally end in 'en'. When the 'en' is removed, the STEM of the verb remains: ('spiel', 'mach'), to which endings are then added depending on the subject of the verb and the tense.

Occasionally an infinitive will end in 'n', rather than 'en'
e.g.   segeln   -   to sail

Infinitives can be used as nouns. They are written with a capital letter and are always neuter (das).
e.g.   Rauchen ist verboten   -   smoking is forbidden

THE PRESENT PARTICIPLE

The present participle of a verb is formed by adding 'end' to the STEM of the verb:
> schlafend   -   sleeping   spielend   -   playing

You are most likely to encounter present participles when used as adjectives e.g. ein schlafender Hund - a sleeping dog.

Present participles are not as frequently used in German as they are in English, and you must be careful when translating for example "is playing", "was playing" into German:

Remember that "er spielt" translates as "he plays, he does play, he is playing" and the imperfect "er spielte" translates as "he played, he did play, he was playing".

THE PASSIVE

Although you do not have to be able to use the passive in German for GCSE purposes, it is frequently used in German, so you should be able to recognise it. A passive construction is one where "something is being done", rather than the active "somebody is doing something":
e.g.
PASSIVE

> der Mann wurde (von dem Hund) gebissen   -   the man was bitten (by the dog)

ACTIVE   der Hund biss den Mann   -   the dog bit the man

The passive in German is formed by using WERDEN + PAST PARTICIPLE

> die Tür wird geschlossen   -   the door is (being) closed (present)
> die Tür wurde geschlossen   -   the door was (being) closed (imperfect)
> die Tür ist geschlossen worden*   -   the door has been closed (perfect)
> die Tür war geschlossen worden*   -   the door had been closed (pluperfect)
> die Tür wird geschlossen werden   -   the door will be closed (future)

*Note that in the passive the past participle geworden becomes worden.

PREPOSITIONS

Remember that prepositions are words which denote the POSITION of something.

In German, prepositions play an important role in the structure of the clause/sentence because they affect the CASE following the preposition.

- For prepositions governing the accusative, see page 61.

- For prepositions governing the dative, see page 59.

- For prepositions governing the dative or accusative, see page 17.

- For prepositions governing the genitive, see page 69.

PRONOUNS

Remember that pronouns are words used in place of a noun, to avoid repeating the noun:

Der neue Schuldirektor ist angekommen. ER ist ziemlich jung.
The new headteacher has arrived. HE is quite young.

- For personal pronouns, see page 9 (nominative only).
  see page 49 (nominative, accusative and dative).

- For relative pronouns, see page 51.

- For reflexive pronouns, see page 19 and page 63.

INTERROGATIVE PRONOUNS

These are pronouns used in asking questions. The following pronouns are used ...

When referring to people:

N	wer	- who?
A	wen	- whom?
G	wessen	- whose?
D	wem	- to whom?

When referring to things:

N	was	- what?
A	was	- what?
G	wessen	- of what?
D	The dative form is expressed by wo-+ preposition	
	e.g. womit schreibt sie? - what is she writing with?	

Man, jemand, niemand
Man can be translated as 'one', 'you', 'someone', 'they' or 'people'. It is used much more frequently in German than the English 'one'.

Man can only be used as the subject of a verb.

Jemand - someone, niemand - nobody

N	jemand	niemand
A	jemand or jemanden	niemand or niemanden
D	jemand or jemandem	niemand or niemandem

Note that in the above examples the accusative and dative forms may be declined; both forms are acceptable in conversation.

The genitive form is rare.

WORD ORDER

There are a number of important rules governing word order in German. Here is a summary of the rules met in this guide:

(i) The verb is usually the **SECOND IDEA** (not necessarily the second word) in the sentence/clause

e.g. ich SPIELE Fußball

mein älterer Bruder SPIELT Fußball

jeden Tag im Sommer SPIELT meine Schwester Tennis See also page 13

(ii) Conjunctions

The following five conjunctions do not affect word order at all:

und	-	and
aber	-	but
oder	-	or
denn	-	because
sondern	-	but (on the other hand)

e.g. er ist vierzig aber er spielt immer noch Fußball - he is 40 but he still plays football. See also page 67

Some conjunctions send the verb to the end of the sentence/clause. Some of the most common are:

als	-	when, as
dass	-	that
ob	-	whether, if
obwohl	-	although
weil	-	because
wenn	-	when, if

e.g. ich hoffe, dass meine Mannschaft gewinnt - I hope (that) my team wins. See also page 67

(iii) When more than one verb is used, or a verb with two parts, something must go to the end of the clause/sentence.

e.g.

- With modal verbs - see page 31, 35 and 43.

  Man kann mit dem Bus fahren - you can go by bus

- In the future tense with werden - see page 27.

  Ich werde im Ausland arbeiten - I shall work abroad

- In the perfect/pluperfect tenses - see page 29, 33 and 55.

  Ich habe ein neues Kleid gekauft - I (have) bought a new dress

- In the conditional tense with würde - see page 37.

  Ich würde einen Computer kaufen - I would buy a computer

- With separable verbs - see page 23.

  Ich stehe um sieben Uhr auf - I get up at 7 O'clock

(iv) Time, manner, place.

The adverbs of time, manner and place must appear in this order in a German sentence/clause:

e.g. Letzten Sommer **(time)**
bin ich mit einer Schulgruppe **(manner)**
nach Deutschland gefahren **(place)**

Last summer I went to Germany with a group from school. See also page 33.

TABLE OF COMMON STRONG AND IRREGULAR VERBS

The following table is not a complete list. Grammar reference books and dictionaries will provide a full list. Compound verbs are not listed e.g. fangen is shown, but anfangen is not.

* indicates auxiliary verb sein in the perfect/pluperfect tense.

INFINITIVE	IRREGULAR PRESENT (er/sie/es)	IMPERFECT (er/sie/es)	PAST PARTICIPLE	MEANING
beginnen	-	begann	begonnen	to begin
biegen	-	bog	gebogen	to bend
bieten	-	bot	geboten	to offer
bitten	-	bat	gebeten	to ask
bleiben	-	blieb	geblieben*	to stay
brechen	bricht	brach	gebrochen	to break
bringen	-	brachte	gebracht	to bring
denken	-	dachte	gedacht	to think
dürfen	darf	durfte	gedurft	to be allowed to
empfehlen	empfiehlt	empfahl	empfohlen	to recommend
essen	isst	aß	gegessen	to eat
fahren	fährt	fuhr	gefahren*	to go, drive
fallen	fällt	fiel	gefallen*	to fall
fangen	fängt	fing	gefangen	to catch
finden	-	fand	gefunden	to find
fliegen	-	flog	geflogen*	to fly
geben	gibt	gab	gegeben	to give
gehen	-	ging	gegangen*	to go, walk
gelingen	-	gelang	gelungen*	to succeed
genießen	-	genoss	genossen	to enjoy
geschehen	geschieht	geschah	geschehen*	to happen
gewinnen	-	gewann	gewonnen	to win
greifen	-	griff	gegriffen	to grab, grasp
haben	hat	hatte	gehabt	to have
halten	hält	hielt	gehalten	to stop
heißen	-	hieß	geheißen	to be called
helfen	hilft	half	geholfen	to help
kennen	-	kannte	gekannt	to know (people)
kommen	-	kam	gekommen*	to come
können	kann	konnte	gekonnt	to be able to
lassen	lässt	ließ	gelassen	to leave
laufen	läuft	lief	gelaufen*	to run
leiden	-	litt	gelitten	to suffer
leihen	-	lieh	geliehen	to lend

INFINITIVE	IRREGULAR PRESENT (er/sie/es)	IMPERFECT (er/sie/es)	PAST PARTICIPLE	MEANING
lesen	liest	las	gelesen	to read
liegen	-	lag	gelegen	to lie (on beach etc)
lügen	-	log	gelogen	to tell a lie
mögen	mag	mochte	gemocht	to like
müssen	muss	musste	gemusst	to have to
nehmen	nimmt	nahm	genommen	to take
nennen	-	nannte	genannt	to name
raten	rät	riet	geraten	to guess
reiten	-	ritt	geritten*	to ride (horses)
rufen	-	rief	gerufen	to call
scheinen	-	schien	geschienen, gescheint	to shine
schlafen	schläft	schlief	geschlafen	to sleep
schlagen	schlägt	schlug	geschlagen	to hit
schließen	-	schloss	geschlossen	to shut
schneiden	-	schnitt	geschnitten	to cut
schreiben	-	schrieb	geschrieben	to write
sehen	sieht	sah	gesehen	to see
sein	ist	war	gewesen*	to be
sitzen	-	saß	gesessen	to sit
sollen	soll	sollte	gesollt	to be supposed to
sprechen	spricht	sprach	gesprochen	to speak
stehen	-	stand	gestanden	to stand
stehlen	stiehlt	stahl	gestohlen	to steal
steigen	-	stieg	gestiegen*	to climb
sterben	stirbt	starb	gestorben*	to die
tragen	trägt	trug	getragen	to wear, carry
treffen	trifft	traf	getroffen	to meet
treiben	-	trieb	getrieben	to do (sport)
trinken	-	trank	getrunken	to drink
tun	-	tat	getan	to do
vergessen	vergisst	vergaß	vergessen	to forget
verlieren	-	verlor	verloren	to lose
verschwinden	-	verschwand	verschwunden*	to disappear
waschen	wäscht	wusch	gewaschen	to wash
werden	wird	wurde	geworden*	to become
werfen	wirft	warf	geworfen	to throw
wissen	weiß	wusste	gewusst	to know (facts)
ziehen	-	zog	gezogen	to pull